WOMEN'S
LIVES

FAMILY HISTORY FROM PEN & SWORD

WOMEN'S LIVES

RESEARCHING WOMEN'S SOCIAL HISTORY
1800–1939

Jennifer Newby

Pen & Sword
FAMILY HISTORY

First published in Great Britain in 2011 by
PEN & SWORD FAMILY HISTORY
an imprint of
Pen & Sword Books Ltd
47 Church Street
Barnsley
South Yorkshire
S70 2AS

ISBN 978 1 84884 368 4

A CIP catalogue record for this book is
available from the British Library.

Typeset in Palatino and Optima by
Phoenix Typesetting, Auldgirth, Dumfriesshire

Printed and bound in England by
CPI UK

Pen & Sword Books Ltd incorporates the imprints of
Pen & Sword Aviation, Pen & Sword Family History, Pen & Sword Maritime, Pen &
Sword Military, Pen & Sword Discovery, Wharncliffe Local History, Wharncliffe
True Crime, Wharncliffe Transport, Pen & Sword Select, Pen & Sword Military
Classics, Leo Cooper, The Praetorian Press, Remember When, Seaforth Publishing
and Frontline Publishing.

For a complete list of Pen & Sword titles please contact
PEN & SWORD BOOKS LIMITED
47 Church Street, Barnsley, South Yorkshire, S70 2AS, England
E-mail: enquiries@pen-and-sword.co.uk
Website: www.pen-and-sword.co.uk

CONTENTS

ACKNOWLEDGEMENTS

With thanks to: Sergio Goncalves Coelho, Wendy Parsons, Marielle Reuser and Julie and Graham Newby, for encouragement and support; and Simon Fowler and Penny Law for valuable editorial criticism.

Introduction

RESEARCHING WOMEN'S HISTORY

Sometimes it can seem as though there are two histories: an active military, political and creative 'male' history, and another invisible domestic history: 'women's history'. Of course, this is nonsense. Women have always taken active roles in history – sometimes in unlikely ways, but these have been less well documented. Fewer women were literate, their achievements were less likely to be recognised and, until recently, they did not have the same educational or career opportunities as men.

You might think that it is impossible to research these 'invisible' women, that their lives went on out of sight and have already been consigned to the dust heap of history, yet this is not true. While women are often poorly represented in the archives, with a bit of creativity and luck, it is possible to find fruitful research sources. In some cases you will use the same sources that you would consult to research men, but you will be looking for different things, often for the stories behind the dates and names. By comparing marriage and birth certificates, you could learn that a woman was pregnant when she married or that she was making a financially advantageous match.

While researching this book, I spent a great deal of time at The National Archives unwrapping fragile documents and discovering pieces of obscure women's lives. I was particularly touched by the story of Amy Gregory, a young married woman in her early twenties, who somehow became destitute in the late nineteenth century. In January 1894, Amy gave birth to a daughter, Frances Maud, in the workhouse, but soon left the institution to try to find work. Amy appealed to local housewives for charity, tramping the streets daily, looking for a job. Alone, penniless and half-mad with hunger, she abandoned Frances in Richmond Park. The authorities soon tracked Amy down, and she was tried and sentenced to death. Her case received a great deal of sympathetic press coverage and the Home Secretary commuted her sentence to life imprisonment.

I traced Amy further through the archives, and discovered that she served just five years at Aylesbury Prison and was released in 1899. She was initially placed in service through a home of refuge in Oxford, but her husband took her home to Richmond instead. Amy wrote to the refuge: 'We are very happy and we have got a nice home here . . . I am doing well, and happy with my husband and my loving children.' In the 1901 census, Amy and James were still living together.

Like any piece of historical research, Amy's story left many unanswered questions: why was she separated from her husband? why didn't she take Frances back to the workhouse, if she could not feed her? While there are plenty of places to research women in the nineteenth and early twentieth centuries, you will not always be able to find the exact information that you are looking for, or may discover something entirely unexpected instead.

In the following chapters I have tried to show what kind of material you might find if you look at wider social history alongside individual lives. I have focused on more recent history, from the 1800s to the 1930s, which has a huge range of archives and resources for researchers. I chose to divide the chapters into types of occupation and social class, because these labels – perhaps more so than any others – were the ones which our female ancestors were conscious of, and found difficult to escape.

While women were excluded from many occupations during the nineteenth century, they constantly entered new ones, for example as doctors, shorthand typists, waitresses and shop assistants. In 1919, the Ministry of Reconstruction reported on the range of jobs that women did:

> Large numbers of married women are known to work in seasonal trades, such as jam-making and fish-curing, as charwomen, as school and office cleaners . . . In many districts married women are largely employed for part of the year in agricultural work, and they are to be found engaged in practically all forms of unskilled and casual work open to women, while they form a considerable proportion of the home-workers.

I felt that it was important to focus on working-class women, as they constituted the majority of the population. A large proportion had to support themselves and their families, and I have included chapters on domestic service, agricultural labour and factory work. These by no means cover the whole range of work that women did, but they do chart conditions and women's experiences in that particular area at the time. Some of their stories are incredibly poignant: for instance, charity worker Frances Power Cobbe's memoirs record the story of two women in late-nineteenth-century Bristol who worked together to make a living using just one pair of sheets and a bit of ingenuity:

> Their sole resource was a neighbour who possessed a pair of good sheets, and was willing to lend them by day, provided they were restored for her own use every night! This did not seem a very promising source of income, but the two friends contrived to make it one.

2

They took the sheets of a morning to a pawnbroker who allowed them, – I think it was two shillings, upon them. With this they stocked a basket with oranges, apples, gooseberries, pins and needles, match boxes, lace . . .

Then one or other of the friends arrayed herself in the solitary bonnet and shawl which they possessed between them, and sallied out for the day to dispose of her wares, while the other remained in their single room to take care of the children. The evening meal was bought and brought home by the outgoing friends with the proceeds . . . and then the sheets were redeemed from pawn at the price of a halfpenny each day . . . This ingenious mode of filling five mouths went on . . . for a whole winter.

I was also eager to present middle-class women and aristocratic women in a different light. These women may not have worked, but they still contributed to society, culture and charity, and left a rich legacy of research sources behind them. This book includes hundreds of examples of discoveries you can make about ordinary women who lived in the nineteenth or twentieth centuries, and I hope that it inspires you to get out into the archives and start researching. Whether you're interested in one specific woman or fleshing out your family tree, there is plenty of information and social history besides the drier facts of birth, marriage and death. I wish you the best of luck in your own research, and I hope that you find the rest of this book useful!

General Sources for Researching Women:

- **Parish records:** If you're searching for a woman who lived before 1837, then check what kind of parish records are available at the appropriate local record office. Find out more about parish records in this excellent guide by Mark Pearsall on The National Archives website at http://tinyurl.com/39nms4o

- **Census records:** These become available to the public 100 years after they were completed. Transcriptions and images of the original census records for England and Wales, from 1841 to 1911, are available from several online genealogy information providers, such as Ancestry.co.uk www.ancestry.co .uk), Findmypast.co.uk (www.findmypast.co.uk) and 1901censusonline.com (http://1901censusonline.com). All these websites are free to search, but charge fees for access to transcriptions or scans. Local and county record offices and family history societies usually hold microfilm copies of returns for the local areas, which may be examined free of charge.

- **Wills:** If you're looking for a will made before 1858, then The National Archives holds over one million wills proved at the Prerogative Court of Canterbury (the majority belonging to residents of southern England), and you will also find some in local and county record offices and archives. For wills after 1858, you must request a copy of the one you are interested in from the Probate Service, which has the National Probate Calendar, an index to all wills made in the UK (Probate Search Room, First Avenue House, 42–9 High Holborn, London WC1V 6NP; http://tinyurl.com/yh7cvwg).

- **Photographs:** Discovering a photograph of a specific woman at a local archive sounds improbable, and in most cases it is, but it is possible to find relevant images if you know where to look. There are special collections around the country, such as Frank Meadow Sutcliffe's pictures of Yorkshire fisherwomen held at the Sutcliffe Gallery in Whitby, or Horace Nicholls' photographs of women workers during the First World War, at the Imperial War Museum.

- **Commercial directories:** These were compiled from the mid-nineteenth century for towns and cities, but some areas such as Liverpool (1766) and Sheffield (1774) have much earlier directories. The first ones list tradesmen by name, and include their trade and address. Later town directories include street listings and private individuals, as well as details of businesses and advertisements. The best place to look for directories for a specific area is at the local record office, but genealogy information provider, Familyrelatives .com (www.familyrelatives.com) has digitised a range of Post Office directories. The University of Leicester has also placed a range of local and trade directories for England and Wales, from 1750 to 1919, online at www.historicaldirectories.org

- **Newspapers:** If you have a rough idea of the dates when something notable happened to the woman you are researching, then it is always worth searching local – and national – newspapers for items on weddings, births and deaths events and even the gossip columns and court reports. For example, Lady Colin Campbell's divorce was reported at length in the *Illustrated London News*. Many ordinary people also had their divorces reported in the newspapers.

  The British Newspapers 1800–1900 online archive from the British Library (http://newspapers.bl.uk) is an excellent resource, and is free to access in libraries and at The National Archives, but you have to pay to download extracts at home. Try local libraries or record offices, and try searching online to find back issues of local papers.

- **Electoral registers:** In 1869, the government granted female ratepayers aged over 21 the right to vote in local elections. This means that, if the woman you are researching owned or occupied a house, business or shop, you will be able to find her name in electoral registers from 1870. The National Archives does not have a complete set of electoral registers, so the best place to find them is in local archives.

- **Divorce cases:** Before 1858, divorce was hugely expensive, requiring an Act of Parliament. Divorce case files contain petitions, certificates and copies of the decree nisi (which gives grounds for divorce, and states when the petitioner can apply for a decree absolute, a finalised divorce) and decree absolute (which gives the names of the petitioner, the spouse bringing the case to court, the respondent and co-respondent – if there is one – accused of adultery with the respondent).

The National Archives holds many divorce records in series J 77, but after 1937 very few records have survived. For a record of a decree absolute, you can request a search from the Central Index of Decrees Absolute from the Principal Registry of the Family Division (www.hmcourts-service.gov.uk/infoabout/family/index.htm).

Divorce cases were often reported in local and national newspapers, so it is worth checking the relevant periods in their archives. Lawrence Stone's *Road to Divorce: England 1530–1987* (Oxford University Press, 1990) gives a useful introduction to the history of divorce.

Chapter 1

WOMEN
IN DOMESTIC SERVICE

From 1871 to 1911, the proportion of women in service rarely slipped below 40 per cent. By 1931, one in four British working women were domestic servants and nearly 5 per cent of families still employed servants, although most households had just one or two. Female labour was cheap and even some working-class families could afford to pay a girl to do the heavy work. Servants worked hard – a 100-hour week was not unusual – and, with no unions to negotiate conditions, some were treated like slaves. Many felt socially ostracised, that they were 'absolutely nothing and nobody', sneered at by factory workers as 'drain 'ole cleaners'.

Despite their massive numbers, over the past 200 years individual servants' lives have been poorly documented. Throughout the early nineteenth century many servants lower down the scale were illiterate, and even after the 1870 Education Act opened elementary education to all, few left memoirs. There are exceptions: Mary Ashford's memoir about her life in service was published in 1842, and Hannah Cullwick began a diary for her upper-class lover in the 1850s.

But how can we research the thousands of women whose lives were unrecorded? It is possible to piece together details of servants' lives from a multitude of places: public records, country house papers, parliamentary reports and hospital patient casebooks. These sources and many more are set out at the end of this chapter.

Women consistently outnumbered men in service, with seven female for every male servant in 1806, and eleven by 1871. They entered service at a young age – the 1871 census shows 710 nursemaids were under 10 years old, and in 1911 over 39,000 13 and 14-year-olds were working as servants. Workhouses and philanthropic institutions such as the Children's Aid Society and the Waifs and Strays Society trained orphans and workhouse children for service. After the 1834 New Poor Law restricted outdoor relief, consigning more families to the workhouse, employers hired ex-workhouse girls, paying them low wages or just board and lodging.

Others, like Hannah Cullwick, went into service locally or took a job around their schooling. Some, like Rosina Harrison, were educated for service.

Rosina's family supported her so that she could stay at school and learn French and dressmaking, rather than go into service lower down the scale and 'be classed for life'.

Why Were Women in Service?

Throughout the nineteenth century, the main careers open to working-class women were domestic service, agriculture, sewing or 'sweated labour' and factory work – or marriage. In 1916, a 26-year-old general servant commented, 'I have come across many girls who have simply married because they were tired of service.' Edith Hall recalled in her memoir of life in service, *Canary Girls and Stockpots*, that in the 1920s her school friends 'became "skivvies" by the fact of them being female and there being very little other work for them'.

For country women, service was an alternative to labouring; a chance to 'better themselves'. In *Lark Rise to Candleford*, Flora Thompson recalled the high hopes for girls going into service from Juniper Hill, the Oxfordshire hamlet where she grew up in the 1880s: 'Neighbours would come to their garden gates to see them off . . . the girl, bound for a strange and distant part of the country to live a strange new life.' Seventeen-year-old Dolly Davey, born near Middlesbrough, escaped 'farm work or factory work' in 1930. In *A Sense of Adventure* she recounts how she became the first local girl to move to London, after answering a newspaper advertisement for a job in service. 'I had to do it, otherwise I'd never have got away. I'd have ended up an old maid, with no future in front of me. There was nothing else but marriage in those days. It was a way out,' she remembered.

Some women had no choice. Mary Ashford was born into a comfortable lower middle-class family in 1787, but when she was orphaned at 12, Mary went into service as she possessed no other skills. Rose Gibbs, born in 1892 in the East End of London, left school at 13 and went into service, 'as my mother had done', because her Boer War veteran father was unemployed. As Kate Taylor's labourer father was often out of work, her family depended on the money sent home by daughters in service.

Although free schooling eventually allowed clever working-class

Most Victorian households employed just one servant

girls to pass exams, family poverty meant that many could not take advantage of scholarships or free school places. Even one child in service provided more security for the whole family, as Flora Thompson described in *Lark Rise to Candleford*:

> As soon as a mother had even one daughter in service, the strain upon herself slacked a little. Not only was there one mouth less to feed, one less pair of feet to be shod, and a tiny space left free in the cramped sleeping quarters; but every month, when the girl received her wages, a shilling or more would be sent to 'our Mum' . . . some of the older girls undertook to pay their parents' rent; others to give them a ton of coal for the winter.

Lavinia Swainbank reluctantly began service as a 'tweeny' (between-maid), in 1922. Lavinia's family could not afford to keep her at school, so instead: 'At sixteen I entered into a career of drudgery, where long hours and very often inadequate food were accepted standards.' Jean Rennie, born in Scotland, gained a scholarship to university in the 1930s, but when her father lost his job she had to 'submit to the badge of servitude – a cap and apron'.

How Did Women Enter Domestic Service?

Throughout the nineteenth century and into the Edwardian era, servants found positions through word of mouth, newspaper advertisements and registry offices, or hiring fairs in more rural areas. Experienced servants could be choosy. In the early 1800s, maid-of-all-work Mary Ashford sometimes looked at nine or ten positions before selecting one.

By the mid-1800s, after girls left school at 10 or 11, they would find a 'petty place' locally. Some began even earlier. Mrs Wrigley from North Wales started her petty place at the age of 7, 'cleaning the floors and backyards on a Saturday for a penny'. At 9 she was a day servant at the local vicarage. In 1841, Hannah Cullwick from Shropshire took up her petty place at 8 years old. A couple of years later Hannah was a nursemaid to eight children, with 'all their boots to clean & the large nurseries on my hands & knees . . . all their meals to get . . . water to carry up & down for their baths & coal for the fire, put all the children to bed & wash & dress them'.

By 1916, the Women's Industrial Council found that most girls began working at around 15 as 'day-girls . . . either as generals or as between girls or under-housemaids'. Others, like Rosina Harrison, trained first in 'sewing and dress-making' and got their first job at 'seventeen or eighteen or even older', and a few were ex-factory workers. There were also charitable institutions to assist young servants, such as the Metropolitan Association for Befriending Young Servants (MABYS). In the 1880s, MABYS found positions for over 5,000 girls every year and checked up on them afterwards.

WANTED, a thoroughly-experienced Superior or LADY-NURSE for three young children for France; must speak French fluently; wages £40.—Reply, by letter only, giving particulars and enclosing copy of references, to Mrs. French, Grosvenor Hotel.

WANTED immediately, trustworthy, Experienced NURSE for baby three years, in Paris; useful help.—Apply Ctess. de Maigrêt, Mansion Hotel, Richmond. Wages £36.

WANTED, NURSE for baby three months old; must be experienced; age between 25 and 35; do own nursery. Apply, giving references and salary required, to Mrs. Ronald Fowler, Norbriggs House, Chesterfield.

LADIES' MAIDS.—Unless you have had the right training in HAIRDRESSING and Marcel Waving you will never secure a really good position.—Expert instruction at the Parisian Hairdressing Academy, 289, Oxford-street, W. (Prospectus free.)

WANTED for South America, Montevideo, LADIES' MAID, Roman Catholic, speaking good English, aged 30 to 35. Write, stating salary, good references required, contract two years, Madame Arteaga, 8, Grenville-street, W.C.

WANTED, CHILDREN'S MAID; three little girls; French or Swiss; good needlewoman.—Apply G., 41, Portchester-road, Bournemouth.

WANTED, French-Swiss CHILDREN'S MAID; must have good English references; good needlewoman.—Apply before 4.30 and after 6.30 at 10, Cleveland-gardens, Hyde Park.

MAYFAIR SCHOOL of COOKERY (Gold Medallists), 28, Craven-hill-gardens, Hyde Park, W.—Lessons daily. All High-class COOKERY and Still-room by FRENCH CHEF. Gentlewomen, domestics, and others quickly trained and SUITED FREE of charge. Board-residence at reduced terms. Engagements guaranteed. Stamp.

GOOD COOK REQUIRED; kitchenmaid kept, six maids, five in family; age about 36; Church of England.—Apply to-day 16, Westbourne-street, Hyde Park.

GOOD COOK and BETWEEN MAID REQUIRED for the country, near Winchester; wages, cook £30, between maid £18-£20.—Write Matron, Sparsholt, Winchester.

Typical late Victorian newspaper advertisements for servants

Fakenham Institution for Training Girls For Domestic Service was founded in 1858, in Norwich. The institution hoped to give pauper girls 'moral training and religious teaching' and to form 'good and reliable servants'. An 1873 report claimed: 'The girls do the whole work of the Institution . . . and take their turns at various employment of Kitchen-maid, Laundry-maid, Housemaid, Parlour maid and Nursery maid; the elder girls also have the opportunity of being sent in to a gentleman's house.' In fifteen years, Fakenham Institution placed 166 girls in unskilled service (forty-seven kitchen and scullery maids, fifty-one housemaids, forty-four nursery maids, twenty-four laundry maids); and 152 as skilled servants (ladies' maids, dairy-maids, general servants and shop girls).

Special institutions trained and placed workhouse paupers, ex-prisoners and prostitutes in reformatories as servants. Employers often paid ex-institution women tiny wages – after all, employing them in itself was 'charitable'. During the First World War, an orphaned house-parlourmaid, placed in service at 15, claimed that many middle-class households exploited ex-institution girls, forcing them to 'work from morn till night without a break . . . cook, wash and do housework, for the magnificent sum of £8 a year'.

Country women went to hiring fairs to find a new place, particularly in the north, until the First World War. Mrs Armstrong, a Lancashire farm servant, found work at hiring fairs during the early twentieth century:

> We used to walk from here to Ulverston . . . the old farmers used to come up King Street and say, 'Is tha for hiring, lass?'
> I used to say 'Aye.'
> He'd say 'What's tha asking?'
> We used to say 'What are you going to give us?'
> 'I'll give you four pound ten.'
> We'd say 'No thank you.' We used to walk on . . . another farmer would come up and say 'Is tha for hiring, lass?' Perhaps we'd get five pound ten off him . . . He used to say 'Can you wash, can you bake, can you scrub?'

By the turn of the century, with better education and employment prospects, fewer young women were willing to hire themselves out. In the early 1890s at a hiring fair, one of my own ancestors, Polly Clarkson from North Yorkshire, rebelled when she was asked to be a home help and was given two shillings and sixpence. She apparently threw it back and said that *she* was certainly not going to go into service! Instead her mother set up a café, where Polly and her sisters worked.

In larger towns and cities, servant registries matched servants with employers – charging both sides a fee. Registry offices were not licensed until the twentieth century and many were inefficient, or at worst, fronts for brothels. Some were known for sending out high-quality servants, like the Mid Shropshire Registry for Domestic Servants, which recruited servants for Windsor Castle. Celia Fremlin visited several London registry offices in the 1930s, while researching her book on life in service, *The Seven Chars of Chelsea*. Celia found that 'The sheer vagueness, muddle, and lack of organisation in the domestic service world is enough in itself to frighten a girl away from the profession.' One registry she went to contained 'an ill-concealed bed with a yellowish counterpane . . . dusty piles of papers, a dirty teacup and saucer and a pair of crumpled up stockings'.

Word of mouth recommendations were the easiest way of changing situation. In the early 1900s, when Rose Gibbs finished a summer place as a laundry maid, her employer Lady Lovelace passed her on to relatives in Dorking. Servants lacking references – or dismissed without them – found ways around it. When she was refused references because her employer wanted her to stay on, Edith Hall 'wrote out a good one myself and gave a friend's name who was in service at a big house and she sent it on for me'. Edith had a support network of fellow servants who could always supply references – and frequently did. Celia Fremlin noticed that her employers rarely bothered to check references anyway, 'I might have been the trunk-murderer, a spy, a leper, a homicidal maniac.'

Checking references could be difficult, especially when most servants were not local. The majority came from outlying districts and rural areas, and went to work in wealthy, non-industrial areas. Only a quarter of London servants were London-born, and in Lincoln, Reading, Coventry and Bath, three-quarters came from rural districts within 20 miles. In 1880s London, one in fifteen working people was a servant, compared with one in twenty-one in agricultural counties such as Norfolk, Sussex and Essex.

Where other forms of work were available, fewer women went into service. In 1851, 60 per cent of York women between the ages of 15 and 21 were in service, but in Preston, which had large textile factories, just 3 per cent were. In 1911, the lowest proportions of servants were found in industrial areas: South Wales, the Midlands, the Lancashire–Yorkshire textiles area, Northumberland, Durham, and southern coastal towns such as Southampton. The largest numbers were clustered in West London, seaside resorts and provincial suburbs. Servants also moved around to gain a promotion or better conditions. In Ashford, of 312 servants in the 1841 census, seven were in the same place ten years later, and only one by the time of the 1861 census.

Servants worked for various strata of society, from dukes and viscounts to 'solicitors, mill owners, shopkeepers, publicans and clerks', and 'carpenters and masons' who 'paid a girl sixpence to clean the knives and books and take out the children on Saturday'. In rural market towns throughout Berkshire, Oxfordshire and Norfolk, one household in six kept at least one maid. In her memoir, *In Service* Rose Gibbs says she began her career in service at the turn of the century in London with: 'a young couple who were only recently married and wanted to be big and able to say "we've got a servant". It wasn't really that they could afford a proper servant, only me as a new maid of all work.' Lower middle-class employers were often relatively informal. Alice Rickers, a young Shropshire maid, who worked at the local vicarage in the late 1800s, had time off around the vicar's weekly bath. 'I used to have to put a big tin bath ready on a Saturday night, which was my night out, and the Vicar then used to have a bath in the kitchen while I was out,' she remembered. Teenage maid Edith Hall disliked living in close proximity to her employers, as she had to listen to their 'wrangling'. One mistress forced her to 'use their old under-clothes as dusters, but as she would not have me wash them first before use, I found the smell of Madam, Master, and polish quite overpowering'. She also frequently uncovered their secrets. When one woman claimed that her husband 'didn't bother her with that', Edith refrained from mentioning the 'naked lady pictures in a little cupboard by his bed'.

Working for the upper classes was an entirely different experience. Wealthy households had armies of servants who were shuttled between town and country houses. The Duke of Bedford had 300 servants in the 1830s, and, at the turn of the century, the Duke of Portland employed 320. Whereas a Hertford bank manager earning £600 a year in 1900 could keep a cook, housemaid, nursemaid and odd-job boy, the Benyon family at Englefield House in Berkshire had twenty-three servants, whose wages cost between £530 and £620 a year.

In the 1850s it became common for servants in larger houses to wear uniforms – blue or violet cotton print morning dresses and light wool afternoon dresses for most maids. Servants usually had to buy their own uniforms. Margaret Thomas complained: 'All we maidservants in that place had to wear black, navy or dark grey whenever we went out, with small black hats or toques . . . Our indoor clothes cost a lot. There wasn't much left for outdoor wear after we had bought them.' Some employers were even fussier. As a housemaid in the 1890s, Mrs Woodburn wore 'grey, lovely silver grey, shiny like alpaca . . . nice plain pinnies, no lace, but happen a lot of tucks round the bottom'. By the early twentieth century, servants wore a 'black dress and apron' and 'faddy mistresses' would also 'require special patterns of caps and aprons'. Lady's maid Rosina Harrison had to dress fashionably, but simply: 'When ladies and their maids were out together there could never be any mistaking which was which.' Even if they had mastered their outfits, some servants found etiquette confusing. Rose Gibbs was a laundry maid for Lady Lovelace in the early 1900s:

> I saw a man with a gun under his arm, so I thought he must be a bailiff. He stopped and asked me whether I had seen his lordship.
>
> 'Yes,' I said, pointing in the direction of the lake. The head maid came out and was furious with me. 'Why didn't you curtsey? That was the duke of Abercorn. You should have curtsied.'
>
> I tossed my head. 'How was I to know who that was? He didn't curtsey to me?'

Rose later worked for the Dowager Countess of Harmonsby, at Box Hill: 'The Housekeeper was in charge of us in the Servants' Hall. Then there was the Cook, then first Parlour Maid, second Parlour Maid, and third. Then the House Maids, first, second and third again. And the Laundry Maids, a Head and a second and I was the third.' Rose's employment ended when she asked for a day's leave to visit her impoverished family in London. Lady Margaret told her: 'I'm very much afraid you'll have to go to London and stay there.'

What Did They Do?

Servants worked in every strata of society, but what did they actually do? Census data shows that servants became increasingly specialised during the late Victorian period. In the 1851 census there were 46,648 housekeepers, and by 1871, nearly 100,000 more, and the number of cooks doubled during the same period. There were also thousands of unclassified servants: 'wardmaids and scrubbers in hospitals, schoolroom-maids in private boarding schools, maids and waitresses in tea gardens, coffee rooms and public houses'.

Housekeeper

During the nineteenth century, the position of housekeeper was often filled by an 'antiquated female, either maiden or widow, commonly an aunt or cousin'. This made sense, as the housekeeper was in a position of trust in upper-class households. Some were married, often to the butler, and, in this case, the two servants might work in the same household. Equipped with a bunch of keys on a 'chatelaine' ring, the housekeeper ran and safeguarded the household, 'securing in different closets and corner cupboards' all fancy glass, china, preserves and linen. In larger houses she had her own room, where expensive stores of 'spices, condiments, soap, candles . . . spirits, essential and other oils', as well as 'household linen, china, glass, pickles and preserves, and cakes, tea, coffee, sugar', were safely locked away.

Other duties entailed hiring and firing lower servants; overseeing the furniture and linen; preparing for guests; ordering goods from tradesmen and making wine, preserves and delicacies such as 'rich, seed cake, a number of pots of currant jelly and raspberry jam'. Housekeeping could be a lucrative profession. In 1772, Sarah Stanniforth, housekeeper at Holkham Hall in Norfolk, left over £1,000 in her will.

H.G. Wells's mother, a former lady's maid, returned to service at the age of 58 as housekeeper at Uppark in Suffolk, because her husband could not support the family. She was, according to Wells, 'the worst housekeeper who was ever thought of', as she 'did not know how to plan work, control servants, buy stores or economise in any way', although 'she knew at least how a housekeeper should look . . . lace cap, lace apron, black silk dress' and managed the servants' hall table with strict attention to etiquette. By 1892, Sarah Wells was 70, increasingly frail, and struggling with her daily duties, as her diary reveals:

Jan 30th: Busy all day – Wrote to Mrs Holmes hoping she will come and suit. What a worry this house is!

Feb 26th: Busy all day indoors. Felt so unsettled, I wish I could get elsewhere.

Feb 27th: Busy as usual all day. Did not move out. No peace with servants here.

Feb 29th: Dairy woman most disagreeable. What a party!

March 26th: I do not feel comfortable, such strange things one sees and hears!

April 23rd: What there is to put up with in this house.

May 28th: Could not get out very busy as usual. Unpleasant comment from the Cook who seems to act very queer.

June 23rd: Did not go out . . . been greatly worried about servants.

August 4th: Twelve years today since I came here and left Beverley. What anxious years they have been to me. What rude insulting people I have had to live with and it is worse now.

Lady's maid

A lady's maid had to be a skilled seamstress and hairdresser, with an eye for fashion. Her duties revolved around dressing and undressing her mistress,

Ladies' maids, like the woman on the left in this picture, were expected to be entirely dedicated to their mistresses. This one, pictured in 1844, helps her mistress get ready for a ball

arranging her hair and cosmetics, perhaps chaperoning her during the day, and repairing and creating clothes. While her duties were less onerous than those of lower maids, they were still demanding. She had to remain constantly 'good humoured & approve of everything her mistress likes' and be ready to '*run quick*, the instant she is *called*' to attend her mistress 'morning, noon and night'. In 1916, one lady's maid complained of the 'long weary hours of sitting up . . . many nights in succession I do not go to bed till the early hours'.

At 18, Rosina Harrison became 'young ladies' maid' to Lady Tufton's daughters. Her duties were light but constant. At 7am, a housemaid brought her tea – a privilege denoting her status as an upper servant. Then Rosina lit the fire; replaced the young ladies' soiled clothes, ran their baths, and made them 'fully presentable'. During the day she was a 'watchdog' accompanying the girls, and in the evening she helped them dress. Later on in her career, Rosina worked for the elegant Lady Cranbourne, and then Lady Astor, the tough first female MP, who sometimes 'shouted and rampaged like a fish wife' at her servant. It was an eighteen-hour job that included five daily costume changes and safeguarding priceless jewels, but Rosina saw caring for Lady Astor as 'the expression of my own life'. And extensive travelling through Africa, Europe and America made Rosina feel like a 'Marco Polo for my class'. After retirement in the 1970s, Rosina wrote a memoir, *My Life in Service*, about her career, which is a revealing insight into the life of a twentieth-century lady's maid.

Cook

A cook was either plain or trained (able to prepare dinners of several courses). In smaller households she might be assisted by a kitchen maid and perform more menial tasks; in bigger establishments she was dedicated exclusively to cooking, with an army of kitchen and scullery maids at her disposal. A good cook had to fit into her employer's routine, as Samuel and Sarah Adams dictated in their 1825 manual, *The Complete Servant*, to 'inform herself of the rules and regulations of the house – the customs of the kitchen – the peculiarities of her master and mistress – and above all . . . acquire a perfect knowledge of their taste.'

When Elizabeth Freeman was employed as a cook by William Cother, a Gloucestershire landowner, in 1837, he expected her to perform a long list of duties to earn her nine guineas a year:

Cook, Roast and Boil Meat, Fry & Boil Fish, Make Pastry, Curry &c . . . obey orders without grumbling. Cut and leave Meat fit to come to Table when cold – make no waste . . . use economy on all occasions. Ask leave whenever she goes from home . . . Have no followers . . . Dinner

Images of a cook maid and pastry cook from Victorian cards

sometimes to be at short notice. Assist the other Servant on all occasions, particularly at Washing, Ironing.

A couple of decades later, Mrs Beeton advised that kitchens should have clocks, as punctuality was 'an indispensable quality in a cook'. She suggested that in smaller households the cook should rise at 6am and prepare breakfast. In larger households, in the morning the cook would oversee breakfast, then set menus with the mistress, and prepare cold food or soups, pastries and jellies for the evening meal, then a light luncheon. The main daily task was preparing the evening meal. And special dinner parties involved a massive amount of planning and effort, as they could run to twelve courses.

Housemaid and parlourmaid

Parlour and housemaids' duties were often interchangeable (confusingly, there were also 'house parlourmaids'). The main division was that parlourmaids answered the door, served tea, and did the lighter cleaning. Housemaids, on the other hand, undertook the heavy work; rising at dawn to light the kitchen fire, they tackled the heavy cleaning before the family woke – beating rugs and sweeping, blacking grates, polishing, lighting fires and heating water. Later on in the day, maids worked upstairs, making beds, emptying chamber pots and cleaning the rooms – polishing, dusting and keeping fires lit. In the afternoons they might 'rest' by sewing in front of the fire. In establishments without footmen or parlourmaids, housemaids had to listen for the front doorbell all the time.

At 13, Ethel Evans became a 'between-maid' for a middle-class family in Shropshire with eight servants. Her daily routine began at 6.30am, when she cleaned 'all the front door steps and the side doors' and the hall. After breakfast, she headed 'upstairs to help the maid' and then 'down at 12 o'clock to help the cook'. She spent afternoons in the kitchen 'doing the vegetables and doing the cleaning'. After the family's dinner at 7pm, she had 'to help with the washing up', and then she would finally collapse, exhausted, in bed.

Kitchen maid and scullery maid

Kitchen maids were slightly senior to scullery maids. Both were usually in their teens, and this would be their first or second job in service. Kitchen maids assisted the cook with skilled food preparation – baking, sauce-making or preparing vegetables. Scullery maids completed more menial tasks such as peeling and chopping the vegetables, and they were mainly responsible for mountains of washing up and heavier work, like scrubbing the floors, keeping the kitchen clean and scouring surfaces with hot water, soap and sand.

Some, like Mrs Woodburn, a teenage kitchen maid in 1890s Lancaster, found the work too hard. Cleaning pans and getting up at 4am to clean the range made her ill, and she was promoted to the lighter role of housemaid. Another kitchen maid at Little Canfield in Essex recalled that her day began at 5.30am. She would black-lead a 6-foot cooking range, light the fire, scrub the kitchen tables and floor, then call cook and upper servants at 7 o'clock (with tea). During the day she also had to 'prepare and cook the vegetables and learn to make sauces, sometimes three or four different ones with a seven course dinner, but, as cook was often drunk, I had to do a lot more'.

In the 1930s, middle-class Celia Fremlin worked 'undercover' as a scullery maid for an elderly aristocrat while writing her account of life in service. Celia was horrified by the lack of privacy, the 'stale boarding school atmosphere', with servants' belongings searched by the housekeeper. She was most shocked by 'the almost superstitious reverence in which her ladyship was held' by the servants, who performed ludicrously simple tasks with utmost ceremony. Celia was disturbed to find that heating up a can of soup for her employer meant that 'eight members of the staff were mobilized':

First the housekeeper (1) came down to the kitchen to tell the cook . . . Then I, the scullery-maid (2) was dispatched to fetch the new tin of Benger . . . and the special enamel saucepan. I handed them to the kitchen-maid (3) who took the lid off and handed the tin to the cook . . . the cook (4) then set to work making the Benger, Now the footman (5) . . . went to the butler (6) for the key to the cupboard . . . Then the footman put the tray on his trolley and wheeled it off to the hall. Here the tray was taken by the head housemaid (7). She took it up to her ladyship's landing and knocked on her ladyship's door. It was opened by the lady's maid (8) who took the tray.

Maid-of-all-work

Huge mansions with dozens of servants were the minority. Most families employed a single maid who worked alongside the mistress, cooking, cleaning and perhaps helping with childcare and the grubbier tasks. Single servants were often lonely. Teenage maid Rose Gibbs 'was left alone for hours and hours' in Fulham, and when her employers went out, Edith Hall was 'expected to stay up in case one of the young children woke . . . I was left plenty of ironing to do and silver to polish just in case I got sleepy'.

From around 1800, Mary Ashford worked as a general maid in London. Her employers varied, and among them were the head waiter at a coffee house, a clergyman's widow, a penny-pinching aristocrat and a West Indian merchant. Mary discovered that some employers were more congenial than others. One woman refused to let her do anything 'that required any art or knowledge' so that Mary would not 'think myself qualified for a better place'. Her pay altered wildly – from two pounds ten shillings a year to ten guineas at the end of her career, but in 1814 all she had to show for thirteen years of service was nine pounds in savings and 'a good stock of useful clothes'.

In the mid-1800s, Hannah Cullwick was a maid-of-all-work. She never felt like a drudge, but was proud to be '4 times stronger' than her mistress, who 'couldn't boil a 'tatoe'. She recorded with satisfaction that she had cleaned 937 pairs of boots in 1860. A typical day for Hannah went like this:

[28 July 1860] Lighted the fire. Brush'd the grates. Clean'd the hall & steps & flags on my knees. Swept & dusted the rooms. Got breakfast up. Made the beds & emptied the slops. Cleaned & wash'd up . . . Cleaned the stairs & the pantry on my knees. Clean'd the knives & got dinner. Clean'd 3 pairs of boots. Clean'd away after dinner & began the preserving about ½ past 3 & kept on till 11, leaving off only to get the supper & have my tea . . . Went to bed very tired & dirty.

Fifty years later, Rose Gibbs' day as a maid-of-all-work in a Fulham flat was very similar:

I was up at six o'clock and often wasn't in bed till midnight. In the morning I had to light the fires and get all the kettles boiling, cups of tea at seven o'clock and jugs of hot water at eight o'clock . . . Before I lit the fire I had to clean the stove, using black lead . . . I had to use my 'elbow grease' before I ever lit it. Then before eight o'clock the dining room had to be cleaned and dusted. Afterwards there was the hall, and even the doorstep had to be scrubbed and the brass polished . . . I had to wait at table, really a parlour maid's job. The mistress insisted that all silver used must be cleaned that same night, and before I went to bed. They often found me asleep with my head on the kitchen table, I was so tired.

Charwoman

By the end of the nineteenth century there were more part-time servants, who lived outside their workplace, and in 1911 the census employment category of 'day girl' appeared for the first time. Living out, daily servants were not permanently on call. Chars were mostly older women, many of them self-supporting spinsters or widows. The 1911 census shows that most were over 35 and widowed. Many had had no trade before they were married, so cleaning was the only thing they could do.

Mrs Wilkinson became a teenage char in 1914:

> I used to do vegetables, and the rough cleaning. There was no hoover . . . I'd to brush carpets, and I'd to take the stair carpet on the lawn and drag it up and down . . . stand on the bay windows and all those tiny little windows I'd to clean every one of them with pan shine . . . my hands were chapped with cleaning . . . Oh, I was generally fed up.

While moonlighting in service to gather material for her book on 'the peculiarities of the class structure', Oxford graduate Celia Fremlin surprisingly preferred the dirt and confusion of charring in a low-class boarding house. Undeterred by the 'overflowing dustbins, pails of dirty water and greasy cloths', Celia was taken on immediately, with no question of references. She soon realised why: 'greasy dinner-plates formed the top layer on the draining board; but below that layers of kipper fragments and biscuit crumbs', and the odd job man 'shaving gloomily into yesterday's potato peelings'. Despite the muddle, Celia enjoyed herself: 'You dropped everything wherever you happened to have finished with it, and when you wanted anything you went to the bottom of the back stairs and screamed. It was most refreshing.'

How Did They Live?

Wages

Servants' wages, like their roles, varied dramatically across the country, and even within individual cities and towns. Unlike factory workers, servants never gained a trade union to standardise wages, and the London and Provincial Domestic Servants' Union, founded in 1890, fizzled out. The main advantage of service was free board and lodging, and some servants received Christmas bonuses, such as panels of fabric. In 1814, board wages at one country house, Ston Easton Park, in Somerset, were a tiny six shillings a week, but the board included 'vegetables from the garden, Small Beer, Coal and Candle'.

Pay was generally better at country houses. Some servants saved up a decent amount of money and goods for their retirement, as the will left by Elizabeth Byron, a kitchen maid at Dunham Massey in Cheshire, who died in 1819, shows:

> First I give and bequeath unto my niece Martha Thomason . . . the Bed with the Bolster and Pillow used therewith, the whitewood Box standing in my Bedchamber, the Chest of Mahogany Drawers . . . my mahogany Tea Board and Tea Table, my Tea Spoons and Tea Tongs and Brass Pestle and Mortar, two of my Brass candlesticks and all my Chinaware.

In the early 1900s, Rose Gibbs earned twenty-two pounds a year – 'a fortune to me' – as laundry maid at a country house. At the end of the century, servants' wages rose by around 30 per cent as they were more in demand, but many employers sought young daily servants who lived at home, to get away with paying tiny wages. This further discouraged women from the profession, as Celia Fremlin noted during the 1930s 'servant shortage': women would be 'wrong in the head' to accept 'an average of fourteen hours a day for ten shillings a week' when they could earn far more in shops or factories.

Female servants often struggled to save money. Prince Albert spoke at the Servants' Provident Society in 1849, on the huge numbers of old servants in workhouses: 'Suppose her to lay by £5 a year . . . when she is settled in a good place, in health . . . but what can that amount to when she grows old.' Less scrupulous employers let their servants work for weeks without wages, and sneakily deducted money for breakages out of their pay. One servant complained:

> Sometimes the mistresses sent their servants away without paying them any wages at all, making up their accounts in a style like this: 'I owe you five and sixpence; but you broke my teapot, which was worth three shillings; and you burnt a table cover worth two, and broke two plates and a saucer, and lost a spoon, and I gave you an old pair of boots, worth at least eighteen pence, so you owe me half a crown; and if you don't go away quietly I'll call the police and give you in charge!'

When Mary Ashford's former employer refused to pay her, she success-fully took him to court. Legal redress was available to servants if employers broke their contract and failed to compensate them. In 1810, Shropshire magistrate Thomas Netherton Parker heard servant Elizabeth Humphries' claim that she was doing the work of two servants without any extra pay. He ordered her employer, Mrs Jennings, to pay Elizabeth one shilling more a week until she had hired another servant.

Rosina Harrison encountered an upper-class 'brick wall' attitude to servants' wages. After five years as Lady Cranbourne's lady's maid, she was 'flatly, almost rudely refused' a pay rise. When Rosina told her ladyship that she was leaving, 'It was as though I had just passed a remark about the weather.' Rosina had a similar experience with her next employer, Nancy Astor. When Rosina asked for more money, reasonable when the Astors spent twice her yearly wage on her weekly travel, Lady Astor reluctantly gave her an extra five pounds. 'I never asked for another rise and I never got one . . . goodness was supposed to be its own reward.' In any case, the law was heavily weighted against servants. A special offence, 'stealing from master' to cover servants robbing employers, was created in 1823, and the highest penalties were death and transportation. Once they had lost their character, it could be hard for servants to get another place. One of Jack the Ripper's victims, Mary Ann Nichols, was an out-of-work servant who had been dismissed for stealing.

Servants only gained physical protection from assault by employers in 1861, with the passage of the Offences against the Person Act. Before that, employers could, and did, legally use corporal punishment on their servants. One maidservant complained to the magistrate in 1800 that her female

Servants had little support if they were suddenly sacked by their employers, and many turned to prostitution

employer had attacked her, saying 'What the Devil are you doing you Nasty Whore,' then pushed her, 'broke her knuckles and sent her to bed'. They were also at risk from other servants. In 1809, Barton maidservant Ann Brown was viciously assaulted and raped by another servant who beat her with a whip, 'kicked her and threw her down and much abused her saying that if she spoke another word he would kill her on the spot'.

The risk of sudden unemployment (Hannah Cullwick was dismissed from Aqualate Hall in 1858 for high spirits, 'playing as we was cleaning our kettles') meant that unemployed young servants were easily tempted into prostitution. Superintendent James Dunlap gave evidence to the Select Committee on the Protection of Young Girls in 1881. Servant girls who were paid low wages, he said, 'come out on errands; they see these girls walking about the streets, their equal in social standing; they see them dressed in silks and satins; they say "You can go and dress in silks and satins, while I am slaving"; they talk to the girls, and they are influenced.' G.P. Merrick, chaplain of London's Millbank Prison, found that out of 16,000 prostitutes he interviewed, 40 per cent had been domestic servants.

Servants had little redress if they were poorly provided for by their employers. The amount and quality of food that live-in servants ate corresponded to how generous their employers were. Mary Ashford spent seven months in the early 1810s being starved by the 'daughter of a Scottish earl', who was 'penurious in the extreme'. A century later, a maid complained to the Women's Industrial Council: 'Our food is bread and butter for breakfast, tea and supper all the year round and our dinner very poor too. We have to pay out something to keep our strength up.' Another claimed that 'poor and insufficient food' had 'completely ruined' her health.

When Rose Gibbs became a laundry maid for Lady Harmonsby she was amazed by the food in the servants' hall. 'When I saw the lovely food on the table, I just stood and cried . . . The butter was made in the estate dairy, the vegetables were home grown, and the fruit in summer included strawberries, raspberries . . . everything you could want.' Jean Rennie, in service in 1930s Scotland, was irritated by the waste of food in the servants' hall: 'I could remember so many hungry children – and here was good food being contemptuously pushed aside.'

Leisure

Many servants only had one day off a month and a weekly half-day, which was very little, considering that most worked from dawn until late at night. In Edwardian Hammersmith, Rose Gibbs had one free day a month 'and that only from 11am to 9pm. Woe betide me if I was late back', but in her next place, had just 'an hour or so on Sunday evenings'.

In 1916, a Women's Industrial Council survey discovered that 'lack of liberty' was the greatest gripe for servants. One parlourmaid said that she had never stayed a year in a place because she could not stand the boredom, 'day after day without being able either to have friends perhaps to see you, or being able to go see them'. A middle-aged cook described service as 'prison without committing a crime'.

Employers were reportedly unsympathetic and even dictatorial. One general servant in the north of England reported: 'A young girl where I live was locked out all night because she was a few minutes late and the neighbours heard her ring and ring again, but her mistress refused to come down and the poor girl spent the night in an out-house on the clay floor.' One Christmas, Edith Hall's employer refused to let her go home and so she had her dinner 'on the draining board (again) by the sink'.

In 1914, 15-year-old Annie Norman was a general maid in Repton in the Midlands. She kept a diary recording her outings – taking tea with friends, walking, cycling and dancing – until her elderly employer forbade such frivolity:

> Feb 1st I went out in the afternoon with Dora on the Willington Road. I met Nellie Williams and Rene R. We then went to Mrs Perry's for tea and then went to Church with Esther Wright, then we went on another walk till 9.15. I then came in.

> Feb 5th I went to the Parish tea at 6 o'clock . . . I had three dances and came back to the Pastures at 10 o'clock . . .

> Feb 15th We had morning tea at 5.15am in bed. Emily went to Church in the morning & I went to Mrs Perry's for tea with Dora and we had some games & then we went for a walk . . . and we all went to Willington for a walk and we didn't half have some fun all 5 of us.

> Feb 18th I went to Esther's for tea and went to visit Mr Wright and Mrs Perry. Ellen was with me & we both went to the rink dancing and came in at 10.15.

> Feb 19th Mrs Singleton said I was not to have another evening at the dancing classes as she did not like to be alone 'poor thing'.

Lonely 17-year-old Dolly Davey, a Yorkshire girl in London, joined the Young Women's Christian Association: 'They were nearly all domestic servants who used to go there. You'd talk about the people you worked for. You could talk about them to your heart's content.' Working as a parlourmaid for a judge in Chelsea, Dolly dusted hundreds of books in his library, which she wasn't allowed to read. 'A lot of people didn't think that you should be educated, if you were a servant . . . I brought my own books, so I kept them in my room,' she complained. Like Dolly, Edith Hall resented this prohibition and would 'steal a few minutes very late at night peeping into the master's books'. But some employers actively encouraged their servants to educate themselves. Louise Jermy's suffragette mistress arranged outings for her and organised reading and piano classes for her in the early 1900s.

Country houses, with their larger servants' halls, often had special facilities for staff. Rose Gibbs enjoyed 'musical evenings once a week'. Lavinia Swainbank, a housemaid in the 1920s, was allowed two free hours every afternoon, 'either to rest or sit in the lovely gardens' and could read books from the library. In the servants' hall there was 'a gramophone and stacks of up to date records, where the gardeners, grooms and under chauffeur joined the indoor staff of maids and footmen for dances after the day's duties had ended. We had a dart board, cards and the ever-popular snakes-and-ladders . . . everything to make a contented staff.'

With so little free time, female servants struggled to find a husband, but it was still possible. Hannah Cullwick's unusual romance shows that while followers were usually discouraged by employers, there were plenty of ways for servants to meet a lover in secret. Just after her twenty-first birthday in 1854, maidservant Hannah met Arthur Munby in London. Arthur was a young solicitor with literary pretensions and a secret obsession with working women – pit girls, mudlarks, scullery maids, trotter-scrapers. Arthur was attracted by Hannah's 5 foot 7 inch, 12-stone bulk and calloused hands, and they began exchanging letters. Hannah was subject to her employers' rules, but found ways to meet Arthur even though she was dismissed three times as a result of their relationship.

Hannah's example shows that servants got away with disobeying the 'no followers' rule. One young house parlourmaid at a suburban rectory wrote to the Women's Industrial Council in 1916:

A good many mistresses object to men friends, why I don't know . . . I live away from my friend and only see him once a fortnight, but my mistress allowed me to change my time out . . . I have refused places because of afternoons out and one lady even went so far as to say that she could not engage me as no followers were allowed.

Lady's maid Rosina Harrison found it hard to keep a boyfriend in the 1920s because her suitors 'would not put up with the haphazard hours'. Having to be back by 10pm 'made every date like Cinderella's ball, only you didn't lose your slipper, you could lose your job'. Yet, Rosina had an ambivalent attitude to marriage. While considering it 'the goal of nearly every women servant', she chose her job over her nine-year engagement. Even so, Rosina and her fellow female servants were anything but nun-like, flirting with local boys at dances and playing 'footsy-footsy under the table' with visiting male servants.

In the 1930s, Celia Fremlin recounted how Irene, the kitchen maid in a London town house, made up imaginary suitors to impress her, although in reality she spent every afternoon off in another nearby servants' hall visiting her sister. She also described a charwoman, who had been dating a hospital porter for five years, 'with steadily declining enthusiasm on both sides': '"I sometimes think I might drop 'im," the char said. "But I don't know how I'd get another. I never seem to meet nobody and I'm thirty, you see".'

Accommodation

Shut in the house all day, once their duties were over, many servants retired to drab attic rooms with damp walls and spartan furnishings. Victorian employers often regarded servants as primitives who were 'only happy if their rooms are allowed in some measure to resemble the home of their youth . . . merely places where they can lie down to sleep'. In the early 1800s, many slept in the kitchen or even cupboards. Later on, attics were used as servants' bedrooms, but these were often cold and 'lamentably ill arranged and furnished . . . cracked looking-glasses, broken basins, and worst of all, bad bedding'. Scullery maid Hannah Cullwick lived in a 'rough outhouse next the kitchen', reached by a coal hole.

In 1933, a working cook, Ethel Beaumont, wrote an article for the *Evening Standard* about substandard conditions she had encountered. One house was 'exceptionally nice – for the owners . . . But the kitchen – there was only a wooden table and two wooden chairs, one backless. There was no fire to sit by, merely a coke boiler and a gas stove.' Rooms and beds were shared, sometimes by several servants. Louise Jermy shared with two girls in a cramped room with 'only just a space between our beds; a long low narrow room, there seemed no air and certainly no privacy'. They were allowed few personal touches. 'A servant's room should have as few articles in it as are consistent with comfort,' advised *Cassell's Household Guide* in 1870. Some employers forbade pictures or personal belongings being displayed, and considered it their right to rummage through servants' possessions.

Servants involved in the 1916 Women's Industrial Council survey complained about sharing with 'four or five girls' to one room, or sleeping in basements with 'no means of fresh air, and only the smell of cooking and drains'. Poor Edith Hall 'was told I smelled, which if true, would not have been surprising as I was not allowed to use the bathroom. I would not have had time anyway.' One servant in a large town house described the inadequate washing facilities for staff:

There was only one bathroom, which we staff were not allowed to use, but when our employers were away we had a special treat of a hot bath every night! Otherwise we maids had a hip bath in our bedrooms, which meant carrying the hot water up . . . We also had a basin, and a jug with cold water. On frosty mornings, the water in the jug had a thin layer of ice on it.

26

In the early twentieth century there were increasing numbers of working women's hostels, and some were specifically for servants. In a pamphlet on English women's hostels, Mary Higgs mentioned how hostels were often refuges for vulnerable young women. One teenage girl who had missed her train was taken to Devonport Young Servants' Friend Hostel after being 'found frightened and helpless in the street'.

Health

If servants became ill or injured through their work they had no legal right to maintenance from employers, and could be packed off without any support. In 1817, Elizabeth Evans had her employer up before the magistrate because she had scalded her feet while working for him and he had refused to pay her wages. Patient casebooks from the University College London Hospital archive reveal the toll that domestic service took. Anaemia, digestive problems and nervous illnesses, caused by lack of fresh air, monotony and long hours, were frequent complaints. The casebooks make depressing reading: Mary Garwood's illness was 'induced by too hard work, as she had to wait on three families'; Jane Smith, suffering from bronchitis, had been 'out of place for the last twelve months, living in poverty, badly fed and clad'.

Young servants were worn out by their gruelling chores. Kitchen maid Harriet Brown wrote to her mother, in 1870: 'I have been so driven at work since the fires begun I have had hardly any time for anything for myself. I am up at half past five or six every morning and I do not go to bed till nearly twelve at night and I feel so tired sometimes I am obliged to have a good cry.'

The End of Service?

Fortunately for many girls like Harriet, at the close of the nineteenth century, basic service jobs for women were increasing. Now they could work as waitresses, cooks, tea-bar maids, in tea shops, restaurants and dining establishments. In 1901, social investigator Benjamin Rowntree discovered that most working-class girls preferred 'to become dressmakers, shop assistant, or clerks, or find employment in the confectionery factories'. One social commentator wrote: 'Where, then, are the girls? . . . they are flocking to the factories, which they embrace as retreats from the thousand and one ills that of late years have come to be regarded as peculiar to their employment.'

Between 1881 and 1901, the number of teenage servants fell by 7 per cent, while those over 45 rose by 20 per cent. Advertising, cheaper transport and better education all reduced the numbers of servants. In December 1899, the *Leeds Daily News* reported that Scandinavian girls were being employed as domestic servants 'on account of the scarcity of English girls'. In 1901, Charles Booth remarked on the 'independent spirit' among the 'lower servants', who turned down positions 'thinking the work too hard, or the neighbourhood too far from their friends'.

Employer Helena Swanwick complained of her servant difficulties, in the 1910s:

> At least four proved themselves abnormally weak-witted . . . One . . . was an irredeemable drunkard . . . One suffered from melancholia . . . [and] was always planning to hang herself. Two turned out to be professional prostitutes; both of these, by the way, were excellent cooks, but intolerable persons to live with. Two others became pregnant . . . and had to be helped away from the men who had misled them.

The shift away from service intensified during the First World War: between 1914 and 1918, 400,000 women left service for factory work and many never went back. In 1919, with soldiers back from the front and many wartime industries scaled down, there was large-scale female unemployment. Women who refused jobs as domestic servants had their unemployment benefits cut. Yet there were still not enough servants to fulfil demand. Investigating the 'shortage', the Women's Industrial Council concluded that: 'The most promising girls are apt to prefer lower wages, less material comfort and much less security of employment in a shop or office or factory work.' Also fewer young women were willing to allow their mistresses to run their lives. After 1939, there was increased demand for female clerks, typists in local and central government, but even in 1951, 22 per cent of working women in England were in some form of domestic service. However, more were in service as daily women. Country houses after the Second World War were hit by income tax rises; many once-luxurious establishments with dozens of staff were now reduced to 'someone coming in for a few hours daily'. Rosina Harrison felt that 'the old order had changed' during the war, with upper classes working alongside their servants, 'No longer did the distinctions of master and servant apply.'

Researching Domestic Servants

Researching female servants' lives is not always as difficult as you might expect. The likelihood of uncovering details on specific women does vary considerably and depends whether they worked on a country house estate – where employers are more likely to have kept records and photographs – or in smaller establishments. For example, in Shropshire Record Office there are records of servants who worked at the Powis estates (1774–1934), including cash books and accounts filled with information about servants.

There are also lots of ways to trace servants in smaller households. For a general overview of numbers of servants during a particular period, take a look at census employment data. You can find census employment figures quoted for several decades in Davidoff and Hawthorne's *A Day in the Life of a Victorian Domestic Servant* (Allen & Unwin, 1976). Census data can also reveal something of individuals' movements between different households and promotions. And looking the addresses up in town and city directories from the same period could help you to discover the locations of houses where servants were employed. The main sources for tracing domestic servants are listed below, but this is by no means exhaustive.

- **Apprenticeship registers (pre-1844):** Servants' careers sometimes began with an apprenticeship, like that of Hannah Cullwick. This was most often the case for children existing on parish relief, who could be apprenticed when they were as young as 7. From 1801 until 1844, overseers of the poor were legally obliged to keep an apprenticeship register for their parish. These are usually held with parish records at local record offices. For example, The National Archives holds the indentures into service of Sarah Southcott, aged 12, and Jane Cox, aged 10, of Brampford Speke, Devon, from 1804 (in series C 108/23).

- **Workhouse admission and discharge registers:** These can show whether women went into service after leaving the workhouse. They include name, date of admission to the workhouse, age, occupation, religion, the parish they were charged to, and cause of destitution. If they were discharged, the register gives the date and circumstances of discharge. Workhouse registers are usually within Poor Law material held at county archives. At Sheffield Archives, for example, there are the official minutes of the Poor Law Union; financial ledgers; reports and correspondence; admission and discharge registers; religious creed registers; registers of births, baptisms, deaths and burials within the workhouse; relief order books; medical officers' examination books and apprenticeship registers. All of these could contain potentially useful information.

- **Newspaper advertisements:** These will often reveal details of pay and employer expectations. For example, the *Morning Post* on 25 September 1914 included the following advertisements:

WANTED CHILDREN'S MAID; three little girls; French or Swiss; good needlewoman.– Apply G., 41 Portchester road, Bournemouth.

GOOD COOK REQUIRED; kitchen maid kept, six maids, five in family; age about 36; Church of England.– Apply today. 16 Westbourne-street, Hyde Park.

GOOD COOK AND BETWEEN MAID REQUIRED for the country near Winchester; wages cook £30, between maid £18–20. – Write Matron, Sparsholt, Winchester.

- **Quarter Sessions order books:** These were created in the Quarter Sessions, where justices of the peace dispensed judgement on minor criminal cases. For most counties, these survive from the seventeenth century to 1972. They record details of cases where servants and employers met in court in disputes over pay or conditions. You can find Quarter Session records in county record offices, some local record offices and the British Library. Cases will often be reported more fully in local newspapers, so don't forget to check these as well.

- **Estate papers:** If the domestic servant you are tracing worked at a country estate or for a large household, then there may be surviving records with details of pay, employment or even dismissal. County record offices have many collections of private estate papers. Try searching the National Register of Archives (www.nationalarchives.gov.uk/nra) search engine, which should pick up holdings at record offices throughout the UK. Estate papers still held by the family will require special permission, if you wish to consult them.

- **Parliamentary reports:** There were several parliamentary reports covering conditions faced by domestic servants. Among the most useful are:

  Report by Miss Collett on Money Wages of Indoor Domestic Servants (1899)

  Report of Women's Advisory Committee on the Domestic Service Problem (1919)

  Ministry of Labour Report . . . on the Supply of Female Domestic Servants (1923)

  Report on Post-War Organization of Domestic Employment (1944–5)

  These can be consulted at the British Library or at some university libraries; a few have been digitised on Google Books (http://books.google.com) and various other websites.

- **Wills:** Employers occasionally left bequests for their servants, and a few servants with sufficient assets left their own wills. In 1831, Catherine Morris, 'bastard, spinster, of Watford, Hertfordshire, domestic servant to Samuel Salter', left a will which is held at The National Archives (in series PROB 31/1292/1018).

- **Museums and country houses:** Many museums and country houses throughout the UK have exhibitions and material on servants' lives, including:

  Erddig, Wrexham: One of the best places to see servant life recreated, with a laundry, bakehouse, stables and smithy. The Yorke family commissioned many portraits of their servants over the years, including a 'spider brusher' woman who had been in service for seventy years (Erddig, Wrexham LL13 0YT).

  Manderston House, Berwickshire: This opulent Edwardian country house, built on an unlimited budget, has extensive domestic quarters (Manderston House, Duns, Berwickshire TD11 3PP).

  Petworth House, West Sussex: A country house, set in a landscaped park, which has large, well-preserved servants' quarters and a cutting-edge Victorian kitchen (Petworth, West Sussex GU28 0AE).

Shugborough Estate, Staffordshire: The servants' quarters reconstruct servant life in 1876, complete with a laundry, a special servants' latrine, and a kitchen stocked with nineteenth-century gadgets such as an ice-cream maker, potato ricer and floor-washing donkey (Shugborough Estate, Milford, Near Stafford, ST17 0XB).

- **Further ideas:** Many domestic service training centres were set up by local authorities after the First World War to divert large numbers of newly-unemployed women into service, an area where there was a shortage of job applicants. Earlier, in the nineteenth century, ex-prisoners, workhouse inmates, orphans and rehabilitated prostitutes were often sent to institutions to be trained as domestic servants. It is worth checking local record offices if you suspect that the woman you are researching entered service through this route.

Servant registry offices were a common source of employment in the nineteenth and early twentieth century. Details of the offices, their locations and sometimes advertisements offering their services can be found in local commercial directories, like *Kelly's*. Many servants ended their lives in the workhouse or required hospital treatment at some point, and a great number of institution records have been preserved. For example, patient casebooks from the University College London Hospital archive are available to researchers by appointment (www.uclh.nhs.uk). Check the relevant local archives to discover whether records for local hospitals or workhouse infirmaries may have survived.

Chapter 2

WOMEN ON THE LAND

T hroughout the nineteenth century, and well into the twentieth, women living in rural areas across Britain did hard physical labour: 'hoeing turnips; weeding and picking stones; planting and digging potatoes; pulling, digging, and hacking turnips; attending the threshing machine and winnowing corn; beating manure; filling dung carts; planting beans &c.' A few were farmers' wives and daughters, others were labourers' wives, struggling to feed growing families, and some were spinsters or widows, labouring to avoid the workhouse. After the 1834 Poor Law ended the system of outdoor relief, more rural women had to work on the land to supplement their husband or father's income. Later in the century, with the advent of trade unions and other industries paying higher wages, male labourers gained better pay and there was less work available for women.

We don't know exactly how many British women worked on the land. Many were seasonal workers and went unrecorded in the census. Just over 144,000 women were recorded as labourers and farm servants in the 1851 census, 58,000 in 1871, and just 40,000 in 1881. In the early 1900s, women were still working on the land, but their numbers dwindled as men and machines took over tasks that the women had formerly done. By 1900, 600,000 men and a paltry 12,000 women worked on the land.

Women of all ages worked on the land, whether they were 7 years old or an arthritic 70. Just like today, there were also hidden costs to women's work. If they had small children, they might need to pay another woman to look after them, and there would also be extra wear and tear to clothes, and more food needed to sustain them. Many farmers preferred to employ single or older married women as they were more independent than women with family demands. In 1867, at Glendale Union in Northumberland, out of 373 adult female labourers, only twenty-nine were married. A large proportion of female labourers, especially in the Kent hop fields and Sussex fruit farms, were between 40 and 60.

The type of agricultural work available to women depended on the area and other local industries. One Poor Law commissioner remarked in 1843: 'The women in one village have always been accustomed to reap, whilst to those of another . . . the practise is unknown.' In eastern England and the Midlands, larger farms had permanent male labourers, and women's employment tended to be seasonal. In the south-east, women and children often worked as day labourers and in gangs. In the west and north, more small farms hired women as farm servants or for seasonal work.

The largest amount of labour available for women was in the north, where a combination of lots of turnip and potato farms – and a smaller population – created higher demand for workers and also provided a better standard of living. In Northumberland and the borders, male farm workers were contracted to provide extra labour from their own families at busy seasons, through the bondage system. The system required married farm workers to house an extra female labourer, a relative or hired woman who was vigorous enough for the hard, dirty jobs, like 'weeding, turnip hoeing, haymaking,

Bondager women were employed as extra hands in labouring families in the north of England

harvesting, filling dung carts, spreading dung, turnip cutting, driving carts and harrowing'. It was not always profitable, though, as labourer's wife, Mrs Anderson from Ilderton in Northumberland, complained to the 1867 parliamentary commissioners: 'I've slaved at the harvest to earn the bondager's money, and left the children without clothes.' While the system had virtually died out by the twentieth century, even in the 1890s there were advertisements in local newspapers for labourers 'with a working family'.

Rates of pay for female agricultural labourers differed wildly across Britain. Broadly, the further north the higher the wages, as farmers there had to compete with the pay at nearby factories and mines. In 1851, average weekly wages for female labourers in the north were eleven shillings and sixpence, but in the southern and eastern counties they were eight shillings and fivepence, and nine shillings and one penny respectively, and as low as six shillings a week in south Wiltshire.

Women always earned less than men, often under half. Some farmers saw women as cheap labour that also enabled them to pay male workers smaller wages, as they could be 'subsidised' by their wives' pay. Within individual farms, stronger, more productive women might command higher wages, and regular labourers received more than seasonal workers. Mrs James Green from Pinchbeck complained to the 1867 parliamentary commissioners, 'I wish they'd tell us how we're to live, when a man's wages won't keep us in bread.'

Why Did Women Work in Agriculture?

As the nineteenth century progressed, there was less agricultural work for women, especially in the south and east, but in the south-west and some parts of the north, women and children worked as labourers well into the twentieth century. Apart from agriculture, there were few ways for rural women to earn money. In places where there were other employment options, fewer women became labourers. For instance, in nineteenth-century Bedfordshire and Buckinghamshire straw-plaiting and lace-making employed many who might otherwise have worked on the land. In Bedfordshire only 3 per cent of women worked in agriculture.

In large families, everyone had to contribute to the family income. It was seen as more important to teach daughters to 'bake, brew, milk, make butter and cheese' than to read. In *Cottage Economy* in 1823, William Cobbett considered that male labourers should ask themselves of a prospective wife: 'Can she bake? . . . if she can, she is worth a pound or two a year more.' Young girls' educational prospects were sparse before the 1870 Education Act introduced free schooling. While there were some opportunities, such as the Christian schools founded by the National Society, ragged schools and Blue Coat schools, these were not widespread. Dame schools, which taught the rudiments of reading, writing and maths for a few pence a week, were also out of reach for the very poorest. Isabella Young from Humbleton told employment commissioners in 1867 that she worked 'in order to send her children to school'. Mrs Aldridge from Barrack claimed that she couldn't send her children to school because, 'they haven't clothes to go in . . . if I can get some reaping they'll go again'. Many girls slipped through the net. Even later in the century, when more girls went to school, their attendance was often disrupted because they were needed at home when their mothers were working or had recently given birth. When almost all schooling cost money, the poorest missed out. Mary Smith, a 16-year-old bondager at Alnwick, did not 'know the name of Jesus Christ . . . could not say what the Bible is'. Anna Angus, a 17-year-old labourer's daughter in Brancepeth, Durham, could not attend school because she had to care for eleven siblings when her mother died. Both girls' situations were extremely common.

Before the 1834 Poor Law, in most areas the Speenhamland system of outdoor relief supplemented low wages from the parish pot. A particularly bad harvest in 1795–6 caused food prices to escalate, and many labourers struggled to buy the produce that they had harvested. To help these families, parishes put the Speenhamland system in place, giving labourers, working and unemployed alike, financial aid linked to the price of bread. After 1834, when the new system ended outdoor relief, many labourers could not afford to educate their children – they needed their wages. Without basic literacy and numeracy, their employment options were limited. However, by 1910, around 92 per cent of the population of England and Wales were literate. In the early nineteenth century, larger farms sprang up across the country. With the passage of the Enclosure Acts between 1750 and 1860, farmers and landowners gradually enclosed huge swathes of common land where local people had grazed animals and gathered firewood. Over 7 million acres – one fifth of England – was eventually enclosed. Crops were cultivated on a grand scale and farmers experimented with the latest agricultural theories. To do this they needed the land regularly cleared, hoed and weeded. And, as the cheapest labour, women were employed to do it: 'weeding . . . winnowing, stone-gathering, sod-burning and todding, scaling, and crow-keeping.' As day labourers, they could be given work when they were needed and sent home when they were not, saving a permanent male worker's wage. Agricultural workers had already felt the effects of enclosure and the industrial revolution – many rural areas losing traditional cottage industries – and large numbers now had to send their women and children out to work. Women who had once undertaken seasonal work to supplement the family income now became day labourers. Everything changed after 1834: under the Poor Law, male labourers no longer had their meagre salaries supplemented by money from parish relief, and if they could not survive on their wages there was only the workhouse to fall back on.

What Did They Do?

The mid-1830s saw a new era of agricultural employment, as observed by the First Report of the Poor Law Commissioners, published in 1835. In Essex there was a 'great addition of females working abroad and the taking of children from school to earn a few pence'. Sussex mothers were seen to carry their babies with them into the fields, 'rather than lose the opportunity of adding her earnings to the general stock'. Young children were frequently dosed with opiates, such as Gregory's cordial, to quiet them while their mothers worked.

One Dorset farmer, Mr Burgess, was typical of those interviewed by parliamentary commissioners in 1843:

> I employ six to eight women all year round. In winter in threshing and hacking turnips . . . at other times in hoeing turnips and keeping the land clean, in hay harvest and corn harvest. In winter they work while it is light, and in spring from eight till six, with an hour and a half for dinner . . . Generally they get 8d a day; at harvest 1s with two quarts of ales or cider . . . Working out of doors is a good thing for women, you may tell them at Church on Sunday by their size and ruddy looks.

The traditional image of women's agricultural work is haymaking: whole families pitching in to gather the harvest. In reality, women performed temporary, seasonal work all year round. The harvest was the busiest time for many farms, and women bound sheaves and gleaned stray ears once the wheat was gathered. Although she had nine children, Mrs Lawson, wife of a farm labourer from Bishop Auckland, 'never missed a harvest for 20 years of her married life', even working while nine months pregnant. Susan Vacher, a 57-year-old widow from Milton Abbas, Dorset, said that local women worked 'in couching, weeding, and keeping the land clean. Generally the regular hours are from eight to five, but at hay-time and harvest longer . . . In harvest I have earned 1s a day and have had two quarts [of cider].'

Day Labourers

Female day labourers did 'all kinds of field work . . . forking corn and filling dung carts, hoeing'. Mrs Henderson, a day labourer at Branton, complained of the 'longer hours and harder work. They now go out at 5.30 and . . . sometimes not back again until 6.30.' In the early 1900s, Kate Taylor's family in Suffolk took any seasonal work they could get: 'stone-picking, sixpence a tumbril load. On Sundays we would go rook-scaring from 6am till dusk for twopence.' Arthur Munby recorded in his diary, having watched 'a gang of twelve stout women and girls', Yorkshire day labourers, picking potatoes near Brotherton in 1862. Dressed 'in white smocks and rustic bonnets and kerchiefs', they worked, 'digging up potatoes with their hands', from seven o'clock in the morning to dusk for a shilling. One told him that they also worked 'at hay and harvest, at pea picking in June, at osier-peeling in May, at tater gathering in October and then at turnip pulling and so on'. She explained that they preferred outdoor labour to domestic tasks: 'in winter we have to stop at home idle . . . and do our bits of household work and sewing . . . Field work is our delight.'

Dairymaids

Women with full-time jobs on farms were often better cared for by their employers than day labourers or seasonal workers. Dairymaids were believed to perform the 'severest' duties, 'milking and making cheese twice a day, and looking after the cheese already made'. But they lived on the farm, were well-fed, and earned decent wages. Dairymaids sometimes worked into their seventies, although few began before the age of 20. They usually worked from 4am to 10pm, without a break on Sunday. Many suffered from 'pains in the back and limbs, an overpowering sense of fatigue most painful in the morning, want of appetite, feverishness'. Mrs Sumbler from Calne in Wiltshire was a dairymaid in the 1830s:

> I had £7 20s a year for wages, with lodging and board . . . The work is very hard in a dairy; when cheeses are made twice a-day, the work is never done; the work lasts all day, from three in the morning till nine at night. The work is very hard moving the cheeses to wipe them twice a-day till they are salted; and once a-week all the cheeses in the loft are moved; these cheeses weigh nearly half a hundred-weight. The work on the Sunday is like that of any other day; things cannot stop. Milking is also very hard work; an hour and a half in the morning, and the same in the evening. The fatigue sometimes is quite too much.

Farm Servants

Larger farms also employed live-in maidservants for household chores, dairymaiding, feeding livestock and extra outdoor work. Florence Stowe worked as a general farm servant at the end of the nineteenth century. Every day she brought in wood and coal, lit the fires, cleaned the house and prepared breakfast. Then she skimmed the milk and heated it for feeding the calves. After that she would 'clean all the milkpans and separator and strainer and milk buckets, swill the dairy', boiling each utensil. 'Each day brought its own particular job, mostly done in the afternoons. One was set aside for churning and making up the butter,' a gruelling two-hour job, weighing, potting and marking up 30 to 40lb worth for market. 'Another afternoon was taken up to clean all the brass, copper, silver,' she recalled.

As a child, Kate Taylor worked as a farm servant for ninepence a week. In her memoirs, she describes setting off at 6am and walking 2 miles to the farm-house, where she did the housework, helped in the dairy, and then delivered milk, eggs, butter, cream and chickens throughout the village. After all that, she was rewarded with a breakfast of 'a cup of cold tea, and two slices of bread from which the butter had been scraped, not spread, on', before starting school an hour late. On Saturdays 'after the milk delivery, there was the dairy, the kitchen and the larder to be scrubbed, and the dining room to be turned out and thoroughly cleaned. Ninepence a week didn't pay for the amount of shoe leather we wore out . . . and we frequently had our feet bound in rags.' Her family could not afford for her to take up a scholarship, so Kate became a full-time farm servant at 13, earning just one shilling and threepence a week, and working for nothing for six months to pay back the cost of her uniform.

Gangs

Kate was luckier than the young girls employed in labouring gangs. The gang system became prevalent after the 1834 Poor Law, especially in Lincolnshire, Cambridge, Norfolk, Suffolk and Nottinghamshire. Small farmers requiring a team of labourers to complete occasional big tasks – clearing fields of weeds, stone-picking or planting and harvesting crops – would make an agreement

Children commonly worked alongside their parents on the land, and some worked in gangs, like these East Anglian children, pictured in the Sunday at Home *in 1869*

with a gangmaster. The gangmaster employed women and children at a small daily fee, taking them from farm to farm wherever they were needed, and some carried a stick or whip to intimidate workers. The 1866 Children's Employment Commission found that some gangmasters pushed their workers 'to the utmost of their strength' to avoid paying another day's labour, and would 'extort the greatest possible quantity of labour for the smallest possible remuneration'.

Gangs usually consisted of very young women and children; the smallest receiving as little as threepence a day. Fourteen-year-old former gang-worker Ellen Brown was interviewed in Lincolnshire, in 1867: 'We first cleaned the turnips and then topped and tailed them. I got 9d and 10d a day. I've been out three summers and two winters. It's very cold work . . . my clothes would freeze round me.'

Mary Ann Gallay from Whimbotsham, Norfolk, worked in a gang from 8am to 6pm in summer and 3pm in winter, stopping 'only about ten minutes for dinner'. They often had to walk 5 or 6 miles to reach the farm first. 'All went,' she told Poor Law commissioners, in 1867, 'little as well as big. I have walked home without my shoes, because we thought it tired us less.' Another young Norfolk woman told commissioners that she had been 'quite broken in health' through working in a gang. The gangmaster 'would not let us go to [shelter] until we were drenched,' she said. 'The man knocked us about and ill-used us dreadfully with hoes . . . He used to "gibbet" some if they were idle, come up behind them, put his hand under their chin, and so lift them off the ground . . . We dared not complain.' Even in the late 1860s, many rural mothers felt that they had no choice but to put their children to gang work, and many accompanied the children. One mother, Harriet Bell, told commissioners: 'I have three girls at gang work, aged 15, 13, and 9 . . . I always go out with my girls when I am able, so as to look after them a bit . . . I would sooner that they were at anything else . . . but, as my children are all girls bar one, I cannot get any other work for them.' Elizabeth Havers spoke in similar terms: 'I call it no better than negro driving or slavery, and can't think it anything better . . . Still poor people must work to get a living, and I cannot see how a poor man with children could do if they were not allowed to work too.' Finally, in 1867, the Agricultural Gangs Act regulated gangs and made it illegal to employ children under 8 years old.

How Did They Live?

Health

Rural manual workers were considered much healthier than city-dwelling factory employees: 'The women working in the fields in this district are very healthy and not so subject to the usual female complaints as household servants,' claimed Mr Brown, surgeon for Glendale Union, Northumberland, during the 1860s. His testimony was in contrast to that of Mrs Gibson, a labourer's wife from the Scottish borders. 'The women are too sore wrought,' she complained. 'Working in the wet is what hurts women . . . My daughter has never been well since; some women cannot stand it.'

Although a few women said how much they liked the outdoor life, others wished that they had an alternative. Some tasks were especially hazardous. Carrying heavy weights while stone-picking could strain the back; yanking turnips out of the ground with bare hands left palms 'reduced to a raw and blistered state by continued friction'.

Hundreds of women working on threshing machines were accidentally mutilated when their long dresses were caught and their limbs chewed up in the blades. The *Stamford Mercury* published a sympathetic report on a threshing machine accident at Yaddlethorpe in 1867:

> A girl named Eliza Stocks, aged 16 . . . had been cutting bands upon the stage, and when they had just finished a smart shower of rain drove the men to take shelter, and some loose straw was thrown over the drum hole and the steam partly shut off. The girl had forgotten her knife, and on returning for it appears that she put her foot through the straw . . . her foot was caught by the drum, which dragged in her leg, smashing it to atoms, and the machine was not stopped until it reached her thigh, then it brought the works to a stand . . . it was more than 10 minutes before the poor suffering creature could be extricated.
>
> Every attention was shown to her by neighbours, the messengers posted off for medical assistance, and the limb was amputated . . . the poor sufferer died at 3 o'clock the following morning. The house in which the parents live is a mere hovel, and their only dwelling room is not more than 10 feet by 12. The family consists of nine persons who have to live in this room, where all the cooking, getting their meals and other household transactions have to be done . . . the corpse was obliged to remain. The body became so offensive on Sunday morning that it was absolutely necessary to remove it.

Few labourers could afford medical assistance, and while some doctors gave free medical help, in many areas the only hospital was the workhouse infirmary. Kate Taylor, who worked as a farm servant in Suffolk in the early 1900s, realised how vulnerable her pauper family was to illness when her labourer father accidentally cut his leg with an axe at work and nearly died from a fever. 'Being a pauper the local doctor couldn't be bothered to attend him,' Kate wrote bitterly.

Leisure

Women's work didn't stop on the farm. Most cottagers also had allotments, and more prosperous families might have a pig, poultry or bees. In 1843, parliamentary commissioners praised allotments as promoting 'happiness, contentment, industry, regularity of habits'. Entertainment was scarce and many women's lives revolved around church, the setting for all the pivotal events in villagers' lives – christenings, weddings and funerals. The vicar also might provide assistance: running clothing clubs or organising entertainments such as harvest suppers, penny readings from popular authors or produce shows. However, sharing a piece of gossip with a neighbour was the main independent diversion many women had.

Later in the period, a few communities developed women's clubs, but for many life was tied to the family fireside. Some were drawn to the inns by the lure of cheap beer, at twopence a pint in the mid-nineteenth century, but only the 'more daring or dissolute' women drank with the men. The tedium of village life was also occasionally broken by feast day celebrations: May Day, Bonfire Night, and morris dancers at Whitsuntide.

During the early 1860s, the superintendent of police for King's Heath, near Birmingham, declared that statute fairs were 'one of the greatest evils in existence. I have seen married and single conducting themselves with the greatest impropriety and young girls, or rather children, stopping all night, dancing and drinking, and allowing the most indecent liberties to be taken with them.' But many fairs were innocent gatherings, with stalls selling 'sausages, gingerbreads, oranges, cakes and sweets. Swingboats and roundabouts . . . visiting clowns and perhaps a dancing booth . . . prizes for wrestling, racing leaping, shooting.'

Dress

Women at work in the fields had little use for the lastest fashions, but many were still eager to dress attractively. William Cobbett complained in the 1820s that 'now-a-days, the labourers, and especially the female part of them, have fallen into the taste of niceness in food and finery in dress; a quarter of a bellyful and rags are the consequence . . . today they are ladies, and to-morrow ragged as sheep with the scab.' In *Lark Rise to Candleford*, Flora Thompson's memoir of childhood in late Victorian rural Oxfordshire, women made bustles by rolling old pieces of cloth around cushions.

Putting together a practical field outfit was equally difficult for many women, especially for those who worked irregularly. Occasional workers often did not possess enough warm or waterproof clothes and were either 'draggled' in 'some thin gown' or bundled up in their husband's coat or boots. While working, women would have perspired heavily, but they also needed to wear enough clothing to protect themselves from wet weather. In some areas, women adopted men's clothes, tucking their skirts into 'long leather gaiters'.

Clothing changed very little over the nineteenth century. For example, women workers at Glendale Union in Northumberland wore 'stout boots, a very short thick woollen petticoat, warm stockings, a jacket, over a washing pinafore with sleeves' in 1867. This had altered very little thirty years later, when they wore 'a short skirt of thick material, stout boots, a large pictur-esque straw bonnet, over a bright coloured handkerchief . . . shawl . . . and oversleeves are tied on while at work', adding 'a wrapper or apron of stouter make' or a lightweight 'slip or pinafore', in summer.

Labouring families often subscribed to village clothing clubs for a few pence a week. At Christmas, wealthy neighbours might donate extra money, and then the total was spent on new clothes for all subscribers, according to the amount that they had put in.

Food

Bread was the staple of a labouring family's diet in the nineteenth century, sometimes costing half a man's income. This would be supplemented by vegetables, small amounts of cheese or salted pork, as well as lard and tea. In poorer areas women staved off hunger with weak tea, and – if they could not even afford that – toast water made from a burnt crust. In 1843, the rector of Bexwell in Norfolk argued that while the 'most careful labourers have bacon, or other meat twice, perhaps three times a week, I have no hesitation in saying that no independent labourer can obtain the diet which is given in the Union Workhouse'. But this was not true of every area.

The 1867 parliamentary commissioners summarised a typical British labourer's diet as 'porridge . . . barley, pea flour, bread of whole meal and fine flour, milk, cheese, and butter, home-fed and cured bacon, and their hot meal during the long mid-day rest'. But they were concerned that the use of tea and coffee was 'becoming excessive, sometimes as often as four times a day', and feared that 'grave evils are resulting from this change of diet'. In the country-side there were fewer shops, and they charged higher prices than in towns, but in the last quarter of the nineteenth century, increasing imports brought cheaper foreign food onto the shelves of even small local shops, and meals became more varied, with tinned meat, fish, jam, coffee and cocoa.

Accommodation

The commissioners considered the diet of agricultural labourers poor, but they judged their housing unbelievably squalid. Alfred Austin, an 1843 parliamentary commissioner, visiting cottages in western England reported in 1843:

Everywhere the cottages are old, and frequently in a state of decay . . .
In the village of Stourpain, in Dorsetshire, there is a row of several labourers' cottages, mostly joining each other and fronting the street, in the middle of which is an open gutter . . . matter constantly escaping

HOME SWEET HOME

Punch magazine *satirises agricultural labourers' notoriously poor accommodation*

THE COTTAGE

Mr. Punch (to Landlord). "Your stable arrangements are excellent! Suppose you try something of the sort here! Eh?"

from the pig sties, privies &c is allowed to find its way through the passage between the cottages into the gutter in the street, so that the cottages are nearly surrounded by streams of filth.

Most labourers' cottages had little provision for cooking or washing. Many villages had communal bakehouses or shared ovens, but some families only had their living-room fire to cook over. Access to water might be 'one or two pumps or wells to cater for the needs of the whole community', and women had to carry heavy pails from the nearest well back to their cottages or improvise by using rainwater butts and reusing their cooking water. Washing clothes was almost unimaginably laborious, with water heated over the cottage fire and then carried outside to a wash tub.

Flora Thompson, the author of *Lark Rise to Candleford*, grew up in Juniper Hill, a rather better class of hamlet in the 1880s, where:

A few of the houses had thatched roofs, whitewashed outer walls and diamond-paned windows, but the majority were just stone or brick boxes with blue-slated roofs . . . Some of the cottages had two bedrooms, others only one, in which case it had to be divided by a screen or curtain to accommodate parents and children . . . the cottages were kept clean by much scrubbing with soap and water, and doors and windows stood wide open.

With the majority of cottages consisting of just two or, at the most spacious, four rooms, space was extremely limited. In Studley, a census enumerator found 'twenty-nine people living under one roof' in 1841. But he concluded that it was 'not at all uncommon for a whole family to sleep in the same room', adding, 'The number of bastards is very great.' In 1845, the Reverend Godolphin from Bryanston in Dorset also criticised the 'promiscuous crowding of the sexes together'. He described the cottages in his area:

the want, in most instances, of anything like proper drainage . . . the foul air which they are compelled to breathe from the too confined space of the dwelling within . . . the old and young, married and unmarried, of both sexes, all herded together . . . I saw in a room about 13 feet square, three beds: on the first lay the mother, a widow, dying of consumption; on the second two unmarried daughters . . . on the third a young married couple . . . A married woman of thorough good character told me a few weeks ago, that on her confinement, so crowded with children is her one room, they are obliged to put her on the floor in the middle of the room.

As late as 1894, labourers were reported to be living 'under conditions which [were] both physically and morally, unwholesome and offensive'. Poor

A cottager's home, as envisoned by F.G. Heath in The English Peasantry *in 1874*

housing was a very real health risk. Doctor Spooner of Blandford treated many rural people for typhus and was struck by the insanitary conditions they lived in. In one cottage he saw 'a large tub containing pigs' victuals' being used as 'the general receptacle for everything'. At the turn of the century whole villages were 'without a drop of water from end to end . . . without even the ordinary conveniences which the law of common decency commands'. Unscrupulous landlords were said to let cottages, while the current tenants 'lay quivering in the throes of death'.

During the early 1900s, Kate Taylor and her large family in rural Suffolk were squashed into 'a living room and two bedrooms' and used a shared washing copper, oven and outside toilet. Even in 1915, the medical officer of health for Somerset discovered that: 'Every variation is met with, from the cottage with an acre or more of land attached, to half-a-dozen or more houses crowded together on a little piece of land without back entrances or even space for the provision of proper sanitary arrangements.'

Land Girls and Beyond

After several shocking post-Poor Law government reports on the employment of women and children in agriculture, the mid-nineteenth century saw public outcry against women having to toil in the fields. The 1867–8 reports from employment commissioners on women and children working in agriculture reflect this view: 'They become rude, immodest, slatternly, and unfitted for domestic service; and when they marry generally make bad wives,' raged one. 'The effect of this constant field labour is that their cottages are in an untidy state, that their families are neglected, and where there are small children, they are left in charge of an old woman,' wrote another, referring to Yorkshire female labourers.

The records of an 1867 meeting of the Norfolk Chamber of Agriculture reveal – to modern eyes – startling attitudes. A Mr Fraser began: 'As to the employment of women in agriculture . . . there has been a great deal of . . . sentimental twaddle on the subject (Hear, hear).' Another 'gentleman' then proclaimed: 'When a poor girl goes to work, then she is contaminated, then she is spoiled . . . if there was a girl more troublesome than the rest, more independent, or more thoroughly good for nothing, she was the girl who went to farm work.'

The 1867 parliamentary commissioners often concurred: 'Few men find regular employment, while women can, being engaged at half the wages . . . Such women have been described to me as "more than half men".' But women defended their choice to work, and even female gentry showed concern. Miss Boucherett, of Market Rasen, a landowner's sister commented:

Field work is often rough, for the girls, but it is not necessarily immoral . . . what has given it a bad name is, that it is the only means girls who have lost their character have of getting an honest living . . . Where the husband drinks or the family is very numerous, they must do more or starve.

But her moderate perspective was in the minority. Some farmers, like Arthur Savory from Evesham, simply didn't believe that women were competent workers:

> Women are splendid at all kinds of light farm work whenever deftness and gentle touch are required, such as hop-tying and picking or gathering small fruit . . . but I do not consider them in the least capable of taking the place of men in outwork . . . Village women, have, too, their home duties to attend to, and it is most important that their men-folk should be suitably fed and their houses kept clean and attractive.

These criticisms followed a general decline in women's employment, which accelerated with the agricultural depression of the 1870s. Men's wages rose steadily and the burgeoning unions, such as the Agricultural Labourers' Union (ALU) formed in 1872, made some headway towards improving conditions. The ALU, however, was opposed to women's employment, with many ALU members arguing that it took work from men, kept wages down and destroyed family life.

Greater use of machinery also made weeding and stone-picking and many other traditionally female tasks entirely obsolete. In the late 1860s, one Nottinghamshire labourer's wife, Mrs Simpson, said to commissioners: 'There's not half the work there was for the women; they sooner take big boys now.' A local clergyman disagreed: 'Everywhere I heard the same story, that women are found to be less and less disposed to go out to work upon the land. They will refuse unsuitable work; they will stay at home on wet days.' By the end of the nineteenth century, relatively few women worked in agriculture. A minority were still hired for short-term seasonal projects, but most needed more permanent employment and took up piecework, washing, sewing and charring. Younger women headed to the nearest urban centre for the factories, shop work or service.

When popular author Henry Rider Haggard toured England in 1901 and 1902, he saw hardly any women working on the land. In *Rural England*, he attributes this to laziness: 'Now Englishwomen will rarely work at all, either at this or at any other class of agricultural labour, that is, unless they happen to be the wives or daughters of small-holders, or can procure light and highly remunerative jobs, just as picking or 'puggling' strawberries or grape-thinning.' Haggard also criticised the tenants on Lord Portman's estate at Bryanston in Dorset:

> In addition to their model cottages . . . the labourers have pensions, clothing and coal clubs . . . liberal allowances in the case of sickness,

allotments, and every other conceivable advantage. Yet they go, and, what is more, strike at hay-time or other inconvenient seasons and are generally troublesome . . . male and female depart, mostly to take service in shops. Few except the 'doodles' remain.

By then, rural working-class women simply had more education and more options. In 1911, landowner Sir Hereward Wake felt that Northamptonshire women were reluctant to labour on the land: 'Nowadays, with their high heels and pretty hats and hobble skirts . . . they are not at all anxious to do any manual labour in the fields . . . I think we have to thank the Education Acts for this alteration in the character of the rising generation of our rustic females.' During the Second World War, there was a temporary resurgence in women farm workers, when the Women's Land Army recruited around 250,000 women to fight 'the Battle for Wheat', but women never worked on the land in large numbers again.

Women's lives on the land were, especially from a modern perspective, indisputably hard, as well as dirty, smelly and excruciatingly dull. Agricultural labourers were also at the bottom of the class system, as Kate Taylor discovered. She resented being expected to defer to village dignitaries: 'I was on my knees scrubbing the doorstep when Lady Thornhill from the Lodge came along. Of course, I should have got up, stood to attention and curtsied. I didn't, but just kept on with my job.'

A large proportion of female labourers did enjoy working on the land, however. Susan Vacher, a 57-year-old widow from Milton Abbas in Dorset, told commissioners: 'I have worked two-and-twenty years in the fields; I am always better when out at work and prefer it to living at home.' As the twentieth century progressed, women workers became an increasingly rare sight throughout the English countryside, as the proportion of cultivated land shrank, and, between 1891 and 1913, 45,000 acres a year went out of cultivation. Today, female agricultural labourers' experiences provide a striking contrast to the opportunities available to modern women.

Researching Female Farm Labourers

- **Museums:** The Rural Museums Network can help you to discover museums all over Britain that explore historic country life (http://tinyurl.com/373mp9s). One of the best is the Museum of English Rural Life (Redlands Road, University of Reading, Reading RG1 5EX). They also have an excellent website (www.reading.ac.uk/merl), which contains plenty of useful information, online exhibitions, and a special guide to the MERL collections. The museum holds a large range of archives and photographs, and you can search their catalogue online.

  Another helpful museum focusing on rural life is the Museum of East Anglian

Life (Stowmarket, Suffolk IP14 1DL; www.eastanglianlife.org.uk), and for farming north of the border, try Auchindrain Museum of Scottish Country Life in Scotland, which preserves a West Highland farming village (Auchindrain, Furnace, Inveraray, Argyll, Scotland PA32 8XN; www.auchindrain-museum.org.uk).

- **Parliamentary papers:** These are detailed, localised sources of information on women's agricultural work, with testimonies from the women themselves. They contain a huge amount of information on wages and conditions, housing, education, allotments and diets. They are available in large city libraries, the British Library and in some university libraries.

  Some of the most informative are the 1821 *Report on Agricultural Distress*; the 1843 *Report from Commissioners on the Employment of Women and Children in Agriculture*; and the 1867–8 *Reports from Commissioners on the Employment of Women and Children in Agriculture*.

- **Contemporary journals and publications**: Periodicals such as the *Annals of Agriculture*, *Journal of the Royal Agricultural Society*, *Journal of the Statistical Society* and the *Farmer's Magazine* all have articles on women's labour, although these are often factual and rarely depict the experiences of the women themselves.

- **Contemporary books:** Published accounts, whether fact or fictional descriptions, from the period you are researching, can be rich sources of local colour. William Cobbett (*Cottage Economy*, 1822), James Caird (*English Agriculture 1850-1851*, 1851) and Henry Rider Haggard (*Rural England*, 1902) all published accounts of their journeys, including a great deal of material on agricultural life. These have all been reprinted and digitised editions are easily accessible online.

- **Farm archives:** are, in some cases, farm records; they are held by county record offices and university manuscript collections. For example, East Riding Record Office has women's labour journals from Saltmarshe between 1801 and 1884; and Hull University holds the farm account books for several farms throughout the 1800s.

- **Earnings:** Some workers were paid part of their wages in kind – for example, in wool, coal, potatoes or meat – and married men usually commanded higher wages than single. For a detailed investigation of agricultural labourers' earnings in 1900, see Wilson Fox's report compiled for the Board of Trade, which is available online at http://tinyurl.com/295uwob.

- **Valuation Office records:** If you're looking into the lives of rural women who were living in the early twentieth century, then Valuation Office records could be helpful. The 1910 Finance Act stipulated that landowners had to pay a separate tax relating to the value of their land, and district valuers assessed properties across England and Wales in 1915. There are plenty of detailed records, including maps and plans. Field books (records compiled after the finished survey) state the owner or occupier's name, their tenancy terms, the valuation, and sometimes details about the property, and a sketch plan. These documents are all preserved at The National Archives and there is an excellent research guide to Valuation Office records at http://tinyurl.com/2vs4ds7.

- **Tithes:** If your ancestors had their own smallholding, then there are far more resources to trace them, although it was more unusual for women to own property, especially in the early nineteenth century. Tithes were a kind of tax traditionally paid to the parish clergy, originally in goods, livestock or produce, and, after the Enclosure Acts, in cash. Individual holdings required to pay tithes were carefully recorded and shown on maps. Copies are held at The National Archives (in series IR 30) and there may also be a copy at the relevant local record office.

- **Vaccination records:** If you get really stuck, then it may be worth searching for your female agricultural labourer in smallpox vaccination records. Vaccination was compulsory for children from 1853 and vaccination registers were kept from 1862. These are usually to be found under Poor Law Union records and contain the child's name, date and place of birth, the name of their father and his occupation. Check with your local record office to find out whether they hold vaccination records.

- **Reconstructing village life:** For an example of how you might be able to reconstruct rural village life through research, take a look at the History House website, which includes a tour around Kelvedon Hatch village from maps, photographs, and census details (www.historyhouse.co.uk).

Chapter 3

WOMEN IN THE FACTORIES

A social worker advised working-class women in 1908 that, if their husband lost his job, 'sit down and cry', because if they 'did anything else he would remain out of work'. But many, especially single or widowed women, had to work or starve, and thousands found employment in factories.

During the early nineteenth and well into the twentieth century, factory workers lived in substandard housing, ate inadequate food and worked long hours in dangerous conditions for a pittance – less if they were female. At the same time, factory work represented a new freedom for working-class women, and, when given the choice, many preferred it to domestic service. A factory job took women 'out of the home, cribbed, cabined, and confined as to space, light, air, ideas and companionship', and provided 'self-respect, self-reliance and courage'.

The first factories in England were the cotton and woollen mills. During the industrial revolution, the textile industries expanded from cottage to large-scale factory production. The speed of the changeover varied across the country. In Wiltshire during the late 1790s, hand spinning had 'fallen into disuse', while in Manchester women still wound, reeled and picked cotton at home for three shillings and sixpence a week. Factory owners preferred workers inside the factory, and in cotton, worsted and flax mills women and children – the cheapest labour of all – worked as machine and frame tenters, spinners, cleaners, carders. By 1835, a single cotton mill might employ 200 people. Gradually, larger, more complex machinery such as steam-looms resulted in more male spinners being employed, with female workers often relegated to unskilled tasks, like carding and tenting. However, in the woollen industry, male and female weavers worked together for the same pay.

In 1896, there were 144,000 factories in England, employing around 1,400,000 women, which rose to 3 million during the First World War. Women worked in flax mills, rope works, glue factories, cotton and woollen mills, sweet factories and dye-works, making everything from boxes to artificial flowers. Factories provided huge local employment. In Lancashire from the mid-nineteenth to the early twentieth century, around half of locals were textile workers, and over half again were women. They were concentrated in

Women working in a Sheffield file-cutting factory, from R.H. Sherard's White Slaves of England *(1897)*

certain areas: in the northern industrial centres – the Midlands, Scotland, South Wales – as well as eastern England and London. The biggest cotton industries were based in Lancashire and Scotland, but some areas specialised in particular products, with Huddersfield producing fancy cloths and Dewsbury heavy woollens.

Unlike most other professions, women worked in factories from the outset, although this did not gain them acceptance from male co-workers. They were paid far less than their male counterparts and, like female agricultural labourers, were viewed as a source of cheap labour by factory owners. Women were seen as occupying 'men's jobs' by male trade unionists, and in the 1920s, passers-by yelled 'Girls taking men's jobs' at London factory worker Edith Hall. Unemployment during industrial recessions hit factory workers hard. In *Home Life of the Lancashire Factory Folk*, Edwin Waugh described the fate of two out-of-work Manchester factory girls when he visited the city in the 1860s:

> One was a short, thick-set girl, seemingly not twenty years of age; her face was sad, and she had very little to say. The other was a thin, dark-haired, cadaverous woman, above thirty . . . her shrunk visage was the picture of want . . . The weather had been wet for some days previously; and the clothing of the two looked thin, and shower-stained . . . Each of

them wore a shivery bit of shawl, in which their hands were folded, as if to keep them warm.

Who Worked in the Factories?

Most employers preferred cheap young female workers in their mid-teens to early twenties, placing advertisements for 'healthy strong girls' and 'families chiefly consisting of girls'. But single women, mothers, widowed and married, young girls and children all worked. In 1832, *The Examiner* published a letter from 'The Female Operatives of Todmorden' in response to an article proposing limits on women's factory work. The female operatives argued that they 'had no legitimate claim on any male relative for employment or support' and that the lack of employment for women, except as 'slaves' in 'servitude and dressmaking', meant that their only alternative was 'to ship ourselves off to Van Diemen's Land on the very delicate errand of husband hunting'.

After the 1834 Poor Law, single women were solely responsible for

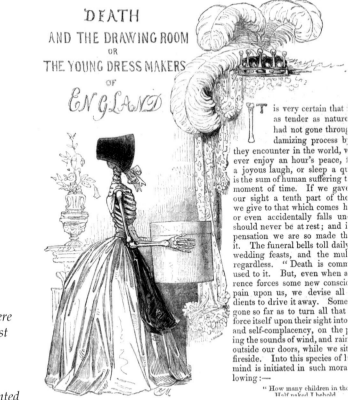

Young dressmakers were among the worst paid women workers, as the Illuminated Magazine *pointed out in 1843*

providing for their children, if they could not face separation from them in the workhouse. While working, some had to leave their children with 'hired nurse-girls, sometimes no more than eight or ten years of age, or . . . elderly women who eke out a living by taking infants to nurse'. Many working-class people feared the workhouse above going hungry, and as late as 1914, a single mother in London was found guilty of cruelty for locking her children in one room while she went to work at a factory. She had believed that claiming poor relief would break up her family.

In the nineteenth century, children as young as 5 or 6 began a lifetime of factory toil. At a pearl and tortoiseshell cutting factory in Sheffield commissioners interviewed Sophia Cockin, who told them:

> I began cutting work at 6 years old. They lifted me on to a stool to reach my work, as I was not big enough to get up myself . . . I was up at 5 and 6 in the morning . . . at work sometimes till 8 at night . . . I have fallen asleep with the work in my hand, and my mother would hit me over the head to wake me up.

Before protective legislation was introduced, workhouse pauper children were often hired out to factories. In 1791, one Yorkshire manufacturer employed 500 children from London workhouses. Children like these were sold almost like slaves, with 'a small premium being usually paid as an inducement', but once there, as factories were frequently remote and there were no inspectors, 'these unhappy little children were often worked almost or entirely to death'. In 1833, parliamentary legislation limited children's hours to forty-eight per week, and gave them two hours' schooling each day, which was extended to the 'half-time system' in 1844. Some employers circumvented this. One inspector found 'the so-called school in the furnace-room, the stoker alternately feeding his furnace and giving a lesson from books covered with coal dust'. The children's employment commissioners interviewed many young girls like 14-year-old Mary Ann Prancer, a match factory worker in Bethnal Green: 'Never was at school in her life. Never went to church . . . Never heard of "England" or "London" or the "sea" . . . sunk in a state of mindless, hopeless ignorance.' But not all working-class girls were ill-educated. Mary Ann Hearn taught a bible class to factory girls in the mid-nineteenth century and was 'amazed at their clearness of thought, their fresh insight'. Only in 1877 were children under 10 completely banned from factory work. Thousands, especially in Lancashire, still became half-timers at the mills in the 1880s and 1890s once they turned 10, and at 12 in the 1900s.

Why Did Women Work in Factories?

In 1889, Charles Booth wrote in *Labour and Life of the People* that 30 per cent of London families could not live on a man's wage alone. In 1921 this was estimated at 41 per cent nationwide, and thousands of women and children were out at work to supplement the family income. Between the First and Second World Wars, married women made up around 10 per cent of the workforce. The Women's Employment Commission in 1919 found many women working to supplement their husband's low wages: 'the same melancholy conditions leading to the same melancholy consequences, the out-of-work husband and the overworked wife with poor health and a semi-starved family.'

Inadequate education usually meant that factory children would be stuck for life doing unskilled work, perpetuating the poverty cycle. Before elementary education became compulsory in 1870, factory children usually missed out, perhaps snatching a few hours at night school. In Oldham and the outlying districts in 1843, in spite of a population of 100,000, there was not one school.

Many working-class girls who gained scholarships had to work because their family needed the money. A Birmingham elementary school log for 1928 shows that although fourteen girls won scholarship places, only four could take them up. Before the 1944 Education Act, which instituted free secondary education, only 20 per cent of children stayed on to secondary school. In *A Bolton Childhood* Alice Foley, a factory worker in the early twentieth century, remembered how her family was able to move into a better house when her sister started work at the mill. She commented, 'Little persuasion or encouragement was available to promising pupils to continue their studies.' Alice started at the mill herself at 13, working a fifty-six-hour week. She got up every morning at 5am:

> Dragging on my clothes and washing at the kitchen slop-stone, then crouching before the fire in a dull stupor, I tried to dry myself on our one damp towel . . . In the oven a pot of strong tea was left to brew from midnight and after a mug of this and a slice of bread we tumbled out into the freezing gloom of unlit streets, amid a clatter of clogs.

Without education or training, poor girls from industrial areas had limited career choices. A weaver in 1920s Lancashire recalled that: 'The only thing we girls had to look forward to . . . [was] getting married and sort of being on our own.' Edith Hall, working in London in the 1920s, was typical of many working-class girls of her generation, and her memoir, *Canary Girls and Stockpots*, describes how she moved between unskilled jobs in factories to unskilled jobs in domestic service, 'leaving each as I thought to better myself, but I never did'. At 19, concealing her working background, Edith went into nursing.

What Did They Do?

Textile Factories

In the first large factories, cotton and woollen mills, women made up a large proportion of the workforce. In 1818, over half of cotton workers were female, some of them small children. The 1831–2 parliamentary committee investigating factory conditions recorded the testimony of 23-year-old Elizabeth Bentley, who had worked at a Leeds flax mill as a 'doffer', since the age of 6, from 6am to 7pm. 'When the frames are full we have to stop the frames and take the flyers off, and take the full bobbins off, and carry them to the roller; and then put the empty ones on, and set the frame going again . . . there are so many frames, and they run so quick,' she said.

A century later, despite better access to education, thousands of young girls were still stuck in the factories. One former teenage weaver said:

> I hated it. I used to tell my mother and she would tell me there was no other work and I would have to stick it . . . The noise used to get on my nerves – clatter, clatter. The times I have been hit with a picking stick. You'd just be bending down, not thinking and it would give you a wallop . . . I scrubbed floors before I would ever go back in the weaving shed.

Mill workers started early – between 5am and 7am – working (after 1802 legislation) twelve-hour days, then (after 1847) ten-hour days. Before this, their hours were at the whim of their employer – shifts of thirteen, fourteen or fifteen hours, or more. Inspectors did not begin to be appointed until 1844, so many employers ignored regulations. A 'factory-woman' from Chorley wrote to the *Working Man's Friend* in 1850: 'Thank God for the Ten Hours Bill . . . [but] the machinery is so rapid in its motion that it turns out as much work now in the ten hours as it used to do in the twelve.' Not all factory owners were unreasonable. One revealed that he had reduced working hours to ten and a half per day, after realising that his workers barely produced more during a twelve-hour day than in eleven. Such long shifts performing vigorous mechanical tasks undoubtedly affected women's health. Especially in the early days, conditions were basic. In cotton factories, dust and debris flew about, causing respiratory problems. Flax mills were damp and humid, and the wet spinning method constantly sprayed workers with water. Cotton factory workers walking out of the factory gates in the 1830s were described by a politician, in *The Manufacturing Population of England* (1833):

> An uglier set of men and women, of boys and girls, taking them in the mass, it would be impossible to congregate in a smaller compass. Their

complexion is sallow and pallid – with a peculiar flatness of feature . . .
Their limbs slender, and playing badly and ungracefully. A very general
bowing of the legs. Great numbers of girls and women walking lamely
or awkwardly, with raised chests . . . Nearly all have flat feet . . . Hair
thin and straight . . . A spiritless and dejected air.

Sweated Labour

Rather than work in the factory, thousands of women did basic industrial jobs
at home, making 'matchboxes, shirts, artificial flowers, umbrellas, brushes,
carding buttons, furpulling, bending safety pins, and covering tennis balls'.
This was known as 'sweated labour' or homework.
  Clementina Black described matchbox-making around 1900:

> One motion of the hands bends into shape the notched frame of the case,
> another surrounds it with the ready-pasted strip of painted wrapper,
> which by long practise, is fitted without a wrinkle, then the sandpaper
> . . . is applied and pressed on so that it sticks fast . . .
>
>   The finished case is thrown upon the floor; the long narrow strip
> which is to form the frame of the drawer is laid upon the bright strip of
> ready-pasted paper, then bent together and joined by an overlapping bit
> of paper; the edges of paper below are bent flat, the ready-cut bottom is
> dropped in and pressed down and, before the fingers are withdrawn,
> they fold over the upper edges of the paper inside the top . . .
>
>   All this besides the preliminary pasting of the wrapper, coloured
> paper and sandpaper has to be done 144 times for 2½d.

Some families worked together and made enough to get by, but the reali-
ties of homework were grim: 'working late into the night; the children kept
from school and pressed into service; floor, chairs, table and the bed used as
receptacles for the piles of half-finished boxes; and the combined earnings of
the family amounting to perhaps 9s a week.'
  Sometimes sweated workers lived and worked with their employer in a
sweatshop. These places were notorious for employing desperate workers
who needed 'employment at any price', then working them to death. In 1843,
Thomas Hood's 'The Song of the Shirt' was published in *Punch* magazine, crit-
icising the exploitative nature of homework:

> It is not linen you're wearing out,
> But human creatures' lives!
> Stitch – stitch – stitch,
> In poverty, hunger and dirt,
> Sewing at once, with a double thread,
> A Shroud as well as a Shirt.

An upper-class woman has a vision of the sweated worker who made her dress in this satirical Punch *cartoon*

Charles Kingsley wrote about the sweatshop underworld in *Cheap Clothes and Nasty* in 1850. Kingsley discovered that sweaters crammed workers into garrets, where 'The foul air of so many people working all day in the place, and sleeping there at night, was quite suffocating.' In one tailoring shop he visited, the sweater took a cut of between sixpence and a shilling out of the price he paid workers for every garment. Each worker also paid him two shillings and sixpence a week for lodging; and another five shillings for tea and breakfast, which swallowed up most of their wages, usually leaving them in debt to the sweater. One told Kingsley, 'We cannot make more than 4s. or 5s. a week altogether.' Soon, in debt and with the sweater owning even the clothes on their backs, they were trapped. Some sweated trades were regulated by the early twentieth century and workers could be independent, 'self-reliant and self-controlled', choosing their hours and making enough money to achieve 'almost a "bourgeois" standard of family life'. Others were virtually destitute, like 'the female "trouser-hand" or slipper-maker', who might earn a shilling a day while working 'twelve or fifteen hours out of every twenty-four', to live in 'a corner of a garret' on a diet of 'weak tea and bread and pickles'.

How Did They Live?

Health

Most factory workers encountered health risks, often extremely severe, and many of them were aware of the risks they took, seeing others in the same job fall ill. They worked long hours in hot and humid or wet and ill-heated atmospheres, assailed by toxic fumes or dust, standing in one position for hours, using unprotected machinery, lifting heavy weights and touching dangerous materials. In 1868, the *Fortnightly Review* complained that factories spewed out:

> miserable objects, many of them grievously deformed in frame, their skins and clothing smeared with oil and grime, the young among them sickly and wan, the middle-aged prematurely broken-down and decrepit, and all so evidently dejected in spirit . . . the very embodiment of hopelessness.

One MP visiting Bradford in 1838 asked to see children deformed or crippled by their work:

> In a short time more than 80 were gathered in a large courtyard . . . no power of language could describe the varieties . . . They stood or squatted before me in all the shapes of the letters of the alphabet. This was the effect of prolonged toil on the tender frames of children at early ages.

At a Sheffield factory, while playing a game with friends, one young girl 'hid beside the drum in a wheel not then working and it was started and crushed her to pieces. They had to pick up her bones in a basket as they found them.' Factory regulation was slow, with Factory Acts and government inquiries steadily accumulating: in 1845, print works were regulated; in 1860, bleaching and dye works; 1861, lace works; 1863, bakehouses; 1864, earthenware, cartridge-making, paper-staining, fustian-cutting. Female welfare superintendents and inspectors were introduced in the early 1890s, intended to act as 'the workers' friend'. Inspectors gradually gained more power and, in 1898, a scheme was set up to compensate workers dismissed after reporting unfair employers. In 1912, when a foreman 'seized, shook and flung' a young girl, unaware that the factory inspector was watching, he was instantly dismissed.

At the turn of the century, there were still many unregulated industries where workers were often horribly exploited. In *The Case for the Factory Acts* Beatrice Webb described unregulated jam-making and fruit-preserving factories at the turn of the twentieth century:

> Scenes of over-work, overcrowding, dirt and disorder, hardly to be equalled by the cotton mills at the beginning of the nineteenth century. Women and young girls are kept continuously at work weekdays and Sundays alike; often as much as a hundred hours in the seven days; and sometimes for twenty or even thirty hours at a stretch . . . puddles

of dirty water on the floor, the clouds of steam in the 'boiling room,' the long hours of standing in boots and clothes made wringing wet by the faulty arrangements of the tubs and water supply.

Serious respiratory problems were caused by the dust-ridden air, 'in rag and refuse sorting, fur-pulling, in hatters' furriers' factories and horsehair factories . . . hemp-rope works, sack-mending, cotton waste works, india-rubber works, eiderdown, clay pipe scouring'. Alice Foley worked as a tenter in the early 1900s: 'The work was done in a basement cellar with no direct day light; the frames stood on damp, cracked floors and I recall that the captive clouds of dust and lint could never escape; they hovered incessantly around the gas jets like swarms of mesmerised insects.' China scourers inhaled fine flint dust. One said, 'Not many scourers live long; we all feel overloaded upon the chest and cough very much; I cannot lie down at night.' Silk workers breathed in silkworm fragments, causing 'a vehement cough and great diffi-culty of breathing'. Workers exposed to asbestos suffered from phthisical, bronchial and gastric problems. Lead workers were prone to fertility prob-lems. In 1922, factory inspector Adelaide Anderson quoted several cases in *Women in the Factory*:

> AB aged twenty-nine, married seven years, had worked in lead ten years, had three miscarriages, five stillborn children, and one child alive who died in convulsions when a few weeks old. CD, aged twenty-five, married seven years, began to work in lead in her seventeenth year, had had four miscarriages and three stillborn children; her one living child was born after she was absent from work.

White phosphorus used in match-making caused 'phossy jaw'; India rubber works had 'naptha fumes, dust lead, great heat and heavy weights'; tobacco workers were poisoned by nicotine; TNT munitions workers had toxic jaundice; licking labels swelled neck glands. Dry-cleaning chemicals caused 'nausea, vomiting and headaches'.

If they avoided the poison, then unguarded machinery could still catch the unwary worker. Accidents were commonplace, especially as machinery was not regulated until the 1840s. Female workers were rarely supplied with appropriate clothing, and their long skirts proved hazardous. In 1894, a 14-year-old fractured her leg in a Lancashire factory: 'She had been at work at a carding engine for several weeks . . . in an endeavour to keep her card in good order by steady cleaning, her skirt was caught in the driving band and the mischief was done.'

One parliamentary commissioner complained that safety measures were rarely taken, even after repeated accidents: 'A woman lately killed in a screw factory from being entangled in the shaft had been caught in exactly the same way at least four times, and in another factory of the same kind three females

Factory machinery on display at the Great Exhibition of 1851

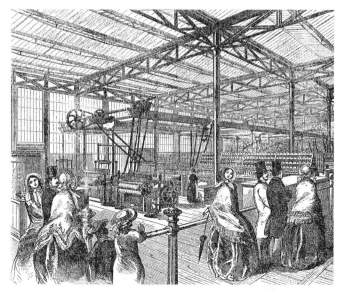

were thus entangled in one day . . . Even when no harm is done the skirts are often torn off.' In laundries, fingers, hands and arms were burned, squashed and crushed in 'ironing machinery, wringers, hydro-extractors'; electric sewing machines doing 3,000 stitches a minute caused septic punctures. In 1913, an inspector witnessed a girl being partially scalped in a machine accident. Manufacturers often resented the backlog of work created when employees were injured. At a Birmingham screw works, in 1864, the manager grumbled:

> We have not had any fatal or serious accidents here, nothing beyond the loss of a finger or so. But there have been several losses of crinolines and dresses from being caught in shafts which run along just in front of the knees . . . it is very awkward for the girl sets up a great screaming, and all the rest do the same.

Some factories provided medical care for workers, but this was usually limited. Courtauld's Silk Mill at Halstead in Essex had a doctor's club, yet 'many of the necessary medicines being too expensive were never given to members of the club'. Often workers had to help each other. At one Nottingham lace warehouse, commissioners discovered that 'whenever a girl is ill and without friends of her own to nurse her, her companions collect money and will give up their own work in turns to attend her day and night'.

Trade Unionism Among Female Factory Workers

Later in the nineteenth century, this kind of support manifested in trade unionism, which was stronger among women in factories than in any other workplace. Women often agitated alongside male co-workers, like the cotton workers in the North East Lancashire Amalgamated Society and the Northern Counties Amalgamated Association of Weavers. But male trade unions were widely hostile to female workers. At the 1877 Trade Union Council Conference, Henry Broadhurst complained that 'wives should be in their proper sphere at home, instead of being dragged into competition for livelihood'. A male trade unionist remarked in the late 1880s: 'When the married women turn into the domestic workshops they become competitors against their own husbands.' Separate female trade unions, such as the Women's Protective and Provident League and the Women's Trade Union League (WTUL), were formed in the second half of the nineteenth century.

The most famous female factory workers' strike was carried out by the Bryant and May matchgirls in 1888. The socialist writer Annie Besant discovered the harsh treatment meted out by the manufacturers and published an article in *The Link* after speaking to several of the workers. Bryant and May punished the workers for the bad publicity, but after they dismissed several workers, 'The women promptly seeing the reason of [their] punishment, put down their work with one accord and marched out . . . some 1,400 women suddenly united in a common cause.' There were many other women's strikes. In 1832, 1,500 female card-setters at Peep Green in Yorkshire went out on strike for equal pay; in 1875, Dewsbury textile workers went on strike; in 1885, Aberdeen jute workers. Between 1910 and 1914, there was a wave of strikes involving female workers. In 1911 alone, there were strikes involving jam and pickle workers, rag-pickers, biscuit makers, bottle-washers, tinbox and cocoa makers and distillery workers.

WE'LL SERVE THE SHOP.

Factory workers were among the first women to be involved in trade unions. Factory workers and shop girls march in this Punch *cartoon from 1857*

The National Federation of Women Workers (NFWW) campaigned for a minimum wage and an end to sweated trades between 1906 and 1921. Their work accelerated the 1909 Trade Boards Act, which set minimum wages in some trades. They also assisted individual causes. In 1908, the National Federation of Women Workers organised a mass meeting for female workers at the Corruganza box factory in Tooting, protesting against wage cuts. The NFWW prevented the wage reductions and the women were reinstated. However, the women's unions were never wholly successful, and even today many women do not receive pay equal to that of male colleagues.

Wages

Women were invariably paid less than men: for instance, in 1898, a girl in a decorated sheet-metal factory earned eight shillings when she replaced a man paid twenty-eight shillings. Edith Hall worked at a record factory in the 1920s, drilling metal disks every day. She felt that male workers were lazier, and resented that they were paid double. One male worker asked her: 'If I get twice as much as you and they are still making a profit, out of me, how much do you think they're making out of you?' One early-Victorian parliamentary commissioner tried to justify this, by arguing that: 'The low price of female labour makes it the most profitable as well as the most agreeable occupation for a female to superintend her own domestic establishment, and her low wages do not tempt her to abandon the care of her own children.'

Despite their unequal wages, factory girls had greater job security than domestic servants, who could be dismissed without warning. But female factory workers' pay varied enormously, depending on the industry, the task performed, the employer and where the factory was located. Early on, workers were generally paid a week behind, and not at all if they were ill. Wages were low in the early cotton mills due to the high proportion of child and female workers – some earned as little as one shilling a week in the 1790s. Twenty years later, Manchester cotton workers' wages depended on skill: while carders earned seven to twelve shillings, skilled spinners could make eighteen shillings.

The 1833 Employment Commission compared male and female factory workers' pay in the Lancashire cotton mills. On average, women in their early twenties earned eight shillings and fivepence, whereas men of the same age earned seventeen shillings and twopence, and women in their thirties were paid just eight shillings and ninepence, compared to twenty-two shillings and eightpence paid to men of the same age. By 1906, it was estimated that a single woman needed at least fourteen shillings a week to live on, but the average wage for women over 18 in non-textile industries was just twelve shillings and eleven pence, and fifteen shillings in the textile industries, whereas linen workers earned just ten shillings and ninepence.

Women were often paid by piece rate and employers could lower the rate if workers earned 'too much'. Alice Foley remembered: 'We had neither work guarantees nor assured wage packets; earnings were brought round each Friday afternoon in individual tins and the money emptied into our palms. Eagerly we counted the coins, relieved if we had a good week, silently worried by a bad one.' Sometimes workers resorted to stealing to supplement their meagre wages. In the 1860s, a Liverpool cigar manufacturer reported: 'We have a female searcher, who now and then stops one, as they pass out; but before there is time to do more, several other girls are round them and a packet of tobacco and cigars is found on the floor beneath their dresses; but no one can say from which it fell.' One Lancashire teenager started work in 1930, on a salary of thirty shillings a week and took on extra work to earn another eighteen pence:

> I used to go three times a week at 6 o'clock. We started at quarter to eight, but I had to go three mornings and get up about half past five and walk two miles to this mill . . . to sweep the looms for my sister, her friend and my own . . . it used to be thick fluff and it was hard work.

She kept two shillings from her wages and gave the rest to her mother, spending her pocket money on Woolworths stockings and going 'dancing round the corner at the village hall'.

Most factories shaved money off women's wages with a system of fines and deductions. Before the 1888 Bryant and May strike, match factory workers were fined threepence if the ground around their benches was untidy, one shilling if matches that caught fire during work were placed on a bench, and latecomers were shut out all morning and lost fivepence. In another factory in the 1890s, girls soldering tins were rarely paid their whole wage, as one penny was deducted for every ten trays of twenty-four tins short of the 190 trays (4,560 tins) required daily. One girl complained to the factory inspector: 'It is slavery. We do not dawdle. We are all scrambling for fear of losing our money.' The inspector made the factory owner refund the money and scrap the fines.

Some fines encouraged workers to risk their health. One girl in a textile factory was fined a shilling 'for letting the web twist round a machine . . . to save her fingers from being cut, and was sharply told to take care of the machine "never mind your fingers". Another, who carried out the instructions, and lost a finger thereby, was left unsupported while she was helpless.'

Food

Many factory workers got by through a precarious system of tallymen and ticket clubs, pawning valuables and making small economies. In the early twentieth century, Lancashire families used the light from gas lamps outside their houses; flour bags became pillow cases and towels; old sacks and coats were used as rag rugs; orange boxes were turned into furniture; old shoes were cut into clogs; layers of brown paper helped to thicken worn blankets; and coal was gathered on railway banks.

Most factory workers ate the cheapest food, but those earning slightly more could afford a decent diet. Dinner for more financially comfortable families might consist of 'meat and potatoes . . . pork, mutton and beef . . . bought and cooked in small quantities', with perhaps a supper of cake or bread and cheese. In 1904, a government commission reported that a 'typical working-class diet' was 'bread and butter for breakfast, potatoes and herrings for dinner, and bread and butter for tea, enlivened by some cheap cuts of meat . . . purchases from the fried fish shop'.

In 1907, one Middlesbrough family of three had a combined income of eighteen shillings and sixpence a week. This was carefully spent on rent at five shillings and sixpence; coal and fuel at two shillings and sevenpence; insurance at sevenpence; a threepence debt; clothing one shilling; tobacco ninepence; and the rest went on food. This family ate:

one dish of meat, tolerably full, about ten inches long . . . seven and a half quartern loaves . . . two wedge-shaped pieces of butter . . . and one piece of lard . . . a piece of bacon the size of a large octavo volume; ten tea cups full of sugar; two breakfast cups full of tea-leaves; four tumblers of milk; a bag of potatoes 16 inches high.

The same amount of food would last the family for two days when they were better off.

Dress

Living on such tight budgets, clothing was a problem for women working in factories in wet, over-heated or dusty conditions. Long dresses and skirts easily caught in machinery, thick underwear was too hot, light material absorbed water or dust. Working-class women had 'very few changes of clothes', so they wore old dresses at home, saving their 'good clothes' for outings. A few who earned higher wages wore good quality fashionable clothes, like one weaver in 1833, who 'very elegantly' dressed in a silk gown, bonnet and silk gloves, which cost over £2 in total. Most had to repeatedly repair clothes. In his 1901 account, *Poverty*, Benjamin Rowntree related how Mrs Smith from York improvised by recycling old clothes:

For everyday wear she buys some old dress at a jumble sale for a few shillings. Old garments, cast off by some wealthier family, are some-times bought from the ragman for a few coppers; or perhaps they are not paid for in cash, but some older rags and a few bones are given in exchange for them. Garments so purchased are carefully taken to pieces, washed, and made up into clothes for the children.

Many spread the cost of buying clothes by ticket systems from shops or hawkers, which cost more but worked out at an affordable shilling or sixpence a week. Some wore extra long skirts because they didn't want to display the worn old boots on their feet. These were often rough clogs or patched second-hand boots acquired from 'boiled boot shops, old clothes shops, market stalls, hawkers' barrows ... begged, found in the street, picked up, patched, polished and sold at a low price'.

Leisure

For most female factory-workers, life outside the factory was almost as tedious as within, and work was sometimes an escape from an even duller existence. Mrs Z, a northern housewife, hardly left the house from 'year's end to year's end' except to shop, as 'it did not occur to her to go out for air and exercise'. There were few public places to accommodate ordinary women. Even if they had wanted to walk the streets, many factory town streets were clogged with filth. Women also had most of the household chores, shopping, ironing, cleaning and cooking, which were organised with depressing regularity. One Middlesbrough housewife's routine in the 1910s went like this:

> On Monday she brushed all the Sunday clothes, folded them up and put them away; on Tuesday she swept thoroughly upstairs; Wednesday she did the week's washing; Thursday she ironed; Friday she baked and 'black-leaded' and on Saturday she cleaned the lower part of the house.

Lady Bell's study of working-class people in Middlesbrough during the early 1900s, *At the Works*, reveals that working-class women did have some fun. The town had four theatres and music halls and a free library. Some women bought twopence theatre tickets to see 'sensational pieces of a melodramatic kind'. They also went to dance halls, clubs and church halls, to the cinema and special working women's clubs such as the Girls Friendly Society, which had nearly 200,000 members nationwide, in 1913. A quarter of the Middlesbrough women that Lady Bell spoke to were 'great readers', especially keen on sensational novels and 'something with a little love and a little murder'.

In the 1920s, young London factory worker Edith Hall used to cycle into the countryside at weekends. On Saturdays, she went to the public baths in Ealing, enjoyed a 'four penny lemon phosphate at Lyons' and window-shopped. Edith was an avid reader, and attended adult education classes, where she was introduced to Thomas Hardy's novels. Reading made her 'feel human and even when my employers talked at me as though I wasn't there, I felt I could take it'.

Accommodation

Factory workers often needed all the distraction they could get from dirty, smelly and insanitary early industrial towns and cities. In the 1840s many Manchester streets were 'unpaved and without drains or main sewers . . . worn into deep ruts and holes in which water constantly stagnates . . . covered with refuse and excrementious matter'. But within these industrial cities, factory workers' housing conditions varied, even within counties, from passable to atrocious. In Barrow, each house had a water tap by the 1880s, yet in early 1930s Manchester over 70,000 tenement houses shared a single tap between thirty and fifty people.

Factory workers could generally afford slightly better housing than the very poorest city dwellers, and many also took in lodgers, usually unmarried working men, to supplement their income. In 1901, York factory workers usually had two to four rooms, but many houses were 'overcrowded . . . old and without modern sanitary conveniences', lacking a scullery, pantry, water tap and privy. Mites, fleas and 'vermin of all descriptions' were common. One Preston factory worker was embarrassed by flea bites, 'You don't want them on your neck and everybody looking at you at work.' Alice Foley's factory-working family lived in a two-up-two-down house, sharing an outside toilet with neighbours in the early 1900s:

> The living-room floor was flagged and sanded, the hearthstone surrounded by gleaming fire-irons. Over the fireplace was a false cornice, a wooden shelf with a faded brocade pelmet. This served to hide a string stretched across the range from which hung damp stockings and handkerchiefs. On top of the mantelpiece stood a pair of china dogs with golden neck-chains, an old clock, and the family tea-caddy.

Those earning lower wages or single-parent families lived in much less comfortable accommodation. Four-roomed dwellings housed ten, twelve or as many inhabitants as could be crammed in. Workers' housing gradually improved, as council housing began to be built after the First World War, and increasingly in the 1930s. All over the country slums were demolished and cheap semi-detached council houses with indoor plumbing were provided for workers.

Many factory workers who fell on hard times headed to the slums. In the late 1860s, Edwin Waugh met a Preston widow with five young children inhabiting 'a dingy little hovel, up a dark court, in one of the poorest parts'. Her unemployed factory-worker husband had starved to death and the family were 'driven from house to house, by increasing necessity . . . The dark,

Benjamin Rowntree visited York slums where unemployed and impoverished families lived, many of them factory workers, and published these photographs in his 1901 book Poverty: A Study of Town Life

damp hovel where they had crept to was scarcely four yards square.' Another family he met had sold all their furniture and 'their only seat' was 'a great stone'.

Some women working away from home lived in hostels. In 1915, in *The Housing of the Woman Worker*, Mary Higgs described their facilities. In Birmingham, Shaftesbury House was full of 'exactly the right kind' of girl munitions worker; the Mission of Love in Liverpool housed seventy-eight 'very poor workers . . . char women, machinists, rag-sorters, tailoresses'. In Oldham, Bent House had a 'varied stream of women and girls needing temporary lodgings'; and Woolwich Ship Hostel had thirty-two beds 'for very poor women'.

Wartime Industries and Women Workers

The outbreak of the First World War initially brought about large-scale female unemployment, particularly in luxury industries. But by 1915, large numbers of women were working in munitions factories, and, after male conscription in 1916, women workers were in demand. Soon they took over factory jobs previously considered 'beyond their strength', working sixty-hour weeks in 'iron and steel works, in chemical works, in brickyards and in gasworks'. In some cases, women were 'selected for their physical strength' and others simply adapted the role, with 'reduced loads, and special steps when stacking . . . lighter tools and appliances'. Women also assumed positions of authority, as managers in 'shell, cartridge, and filling factories . . . from general engineering to jewellery and tobacco'.

R.M. Burridge wrote to her old college magazine in 1916 about her munitions work at Woolwich Arsenal. She trained in 'ammunition of all sorts, filling shells, methods of dealing with high explosives', and to begin with, 'I found the work most boring and kept thinking "What a frightful waste of time" . . . but after a bit I got out of that way of looking at the job and now I can get quite keen on the day's work.' After completing her training, Miss Burridge joined the Woolwich Arsenal as an inspector in a shed of 350 men and ten girls. The women workers were at first 'much disliked by our fellow-workmen . . . they saw no reason to have us at all', but after three weeks, 100 more girls joined and the men had to accept their new workmates. Middle-class Miss Burridge found herself rubbing shoulders with 'all sorts and conditions of men (and women) . . . The workers are very jolly and always ready to help each other,' she wrote, 'though keen competition exists as to who can turn out the most work in a day' or gain a prize for the 'best kept lathe'.

But her daily duties were fairly dull:

I have to see that they are not late, start the motor in the morning, and see the work well started . . . set the tools when required, generally several times a day, then collect all the day before's output and gauge it all to the thousandth part of an inch . . . being scolded by 'the guv'nor' and passing on bits of the scoldings to the shift . . . some days I feel there is more than I can do . . . [but] I am glad of a chance to help 'carry on' though it's only a little bit.

Many newly-skilled women working in factories lost their jobs when ex-soldiers returned, like Mrs Peters, a Lancashire weaver who had been promoted from the factory floor to a clerking position. Women who wanted to continue working were considered unpatriotic – 'Girls taking men's jobs.' But in some areas, such as Cowley in Oxford and parts of South Wales, new factories appeared, specialising in electrical components, bulbs, sanitary towels and cosmetics, and these often employed women. The rayon industry alone employed over 10,000 women by 1936. In 1919, more than 600,000 women were registered as unemployed. They encountered snobbish attitudes from those administering benefits who felt that it was part of their job to comment on applicants' moral character. One refused to recommend Cathie Wothergroon, a 19-year-old Glaswegian paper worker for domestic service because she had 'peroxide hair, plucked eyebrows and make up' and 'paste earrings'. The report concluded: 'Very poor and unsatisfactory type.'

Many more women were unregistered, as unemployed women who refused jobs as domestic servants were denied benefits. The Society of Women Welders complained that skilled women were wasted in basic roles, but domestic service was the only retraining scheme offered to women in the 1920s and 1930s.

In *Canary Girls and Stockpots* Edith Hall, a London factory worker in the 1920s, listed the seventeen jobs she had as a teenager, including production line jobs in electrical engineering; metalworking and in a sweet factory; short stints in domestic service and as a shop assistant; and a brief incarnation as a factory tea trolley girl. Her memories of the sweet factory reveal a bright young girl performing a robotic task:

The machines covered creams and toffees with chocolate and it was a very boring job to keep the travelling belt always filled with creams. We were allowed eight minutes for refreshments and we used to take Oxo cubes to make a hot drink. But my young fellow-worker, Molly and myself broke the monotony by putting out meat cubes on the enrobing machines, and getting them covered with chocolate. We thought it funny imagining the 'tart' and her 'feller' in the pictures biting into the meat cube covered in chocolate. Molly and I used to be at that machine 10 hours a day sometimes.

Afterwards . . .

While thousands were still trapped in boring jobs, attitudes were shifting. Women had proved that they could work in 'men's jobs' and their acheivements carried over to peacetime in some respects. The Ministry of Reconstruction reported in 1919: 'The driving of taxi-cabs on our London streets is just as suitable for women as the driving of official cars.' Victorian women had mostly been driven to factory work by necessity; after all, there were few alternatives – poverty, prostitution, sweated work or domestic service, but their daughters and granddaughters had more choices. Various factors combined in the early twentieth century to give women more options.

Throughout the mid-1800s, the Factory Acts limited children's labour and the 1870 Education Act provided free elementary education. The 1890s saw a huge range of new opportunities for women – as waitresses and office clerks, in the Civil Service or Post Office. In 1910, a male bookbinder commented that young girls were no longer eager to enter the trade as they were set on becoming 'a type-writer or a waitress' instead.

During the First World War, women acquired the training to replace skilled male factory workers. In the London engineering trade in 1891, one worker in fifty was female, but there were ten times this by 1929. With women gaining the vote, working in what had traditionally been 'men's jobs', and even wearing trousers, the campaign for equal pay began to look achievable.

Researching Female Factory Workers

- **Business records:** These can often provide a few interesting hints or, if you are lucky, lengthy details on a woman's employment with a particular company. To start searching business records you need to know exactly where they are held. Try searching the National Register of Archives (www.nationalarchives .gov.uk/nra/default.asp), enquire at local or county record offices, and ask the firms themselves, if they still exist. If they do not, then it is worth looking up the history of the firm to find out whether the business was bought out by a firm that is still running. For example, JS Fry and Sons were acquired by Cadburys.

- **The Women's Industrial Council:** This organisation collected information on working women in over 100 different trades and, in 1915, Clementina Black published it in her book *Married Women's Work*, intending to encourage government legislation to protect women workers. The Women's Industrial Council printed archive is held at the Trade Union Library at London Metropolitan University (Trades Union Congress Library Collections, Holloway Road Learning Centre, 236–50 Holloway Road, London N7 6PP). It also holds the records of the Women's Trade Union League (1895–1921).

- **Trade Union records:** These are often held locally, by existing trade unions or have been passed on to local libraries and archives. There are also several excellent centres for trade union records, including:

The Modern Records Centre at Warwick University (Modern Records Centre, University Library, University of Warwick, Coventry CV4 7AL; www2 .warwick.ac.uk/services/library/mrc).

The Labour History Archive, based at the People's History Museum in Manchester. This has a large collection of trade union and socialist material (Labour History Archive, People's History Museum, Left Bank, Spinningfields, Manchester M3 3ER; www.phm.org.uk/archive-study-centre).

The Women's Library (The Women's Library, London Metropolitan University, 25 Old Castle Street, London E1 7NT; www.londonmet.ac.uk/ thewomenslibrary). This has a large collection of women's trade union material – from books to postcards and banners. Among the holdings are the papers of the Women's Employment Federation (1910–79), the private papers of important female trade unionists, press cuttings and various scrapbooks on women's working conditions.

The Working Class Movement Library, Salford (Working Class Movement Library, 51 The Crescent, Salford M5 4WX; www.wcml.org.uk). This holds material on trades unions from the 1820s onwards, with contemporary material – records kept by the unions such as agendas, minutes and publications – as well as plenty of biographies, memoirs and histories.

- **Parliamentary papers:** These contain detailed reports by government commissions and often direct evidence from women workers, but do be aware that they can reflect the prejudices of the period. Some of the most significant topics and the corresponding reports are:

Woollen trade and manufacture (1802–3, vols V and VII; 1806, vol. III; 1828, vol. VIII)

Cotton manufacture (1802–3, vol. VIII; 1808, vol. II; 1809, vol. III; 1810–11, vol. II)

Weavers (1805, vol. III; 1834, vol. X; 1835, vols XIII and XLII; 1840, vol. XXIII; 1841, vol. X)

Child workers (1816, vol. III; 1831–2, vol. XV; 1843, vol. XV; 1865, vol. XX)

Factory inspectors' reports include some of the most valuable testimony from workers. Although parliamentary papers are difficult to find outside the British Library and larger city and university libraries, a few have been scanned and made available on the internet, for example on Google Books (http://books .google.com) and it is worth searching to check whether any you are interested in have been digitised.

- **Periodicals:** There are many periodicals for working women, and trade union organs, such as *The Woman Worker* (1907–921), *Women's Industrial News* (1895–1919), as well as many more localised or specialised ones, such as *The Woman Engineer*. Some publications will be available from local libraries and record offices, but the British Library, the Women's Library and university libraries are the best places to find them.

- **Museums:** For a flavour of industrial life, try the People's History Museum in Manchester (Left Bank, Spinningfields, Manchester M3 3ER; www.phm.org.uk) or the Glasgow People's Palace (People's Palace and Winter Gardens, Glasgow Green, Glasgow G40 1AT; www.glasgowlife.org.uk/museums).

Chapter 4

MIDDLE-CLASS WOMEN

Victorian middle-class girls were not supposed to have lives of their own. 'A boy might be a person, but not a girl,' reflected Helena Swanwick, a talented Cambridge graduate, whose mother read her letters until she married at 24. Lack of personal space was compounded by the dreary domestic routine open to most middle-class women. During his social investigation of York in the early twentieth century, *Poverty: A Study of Town Life*, Benjamin Rowntree observed that middle-class women were often more restricted than working women: 'Left in the house all day whilst their husbands are at work . . . in the deadening monotony of their lives these women too often become mere hopeless drudges . . . nurse, cook, housemaid all in one.' In Edwardian Cambridge, while their husbands wrote and lectured, the 'really important' weekly task for dons' wives was 'going to London for the day to shop'.

While many middle-class women worked behind the scenes in male

An idealised image of the Victorian middle-class family, from Mrs L.G. Abell, Gems by the Way-Side: An Offering of Purity and Truth *(1878)*

relatives' businesses, far more women did, as Florence Nightingale put it, 'a bit of this and a bit of that' at home. Some, like 20-year-old Amy Pearce from Gloucester, enjoyed their quiet, homely lives. Amy recorded her simple routine in a diary during the 1870s: 'What with the children's lessons, the dress-making, practising reading, & going out, I scarcely ever have an idle moment, & I am very glad of it.' Others, like Edwardian teenager Katharine Chorley, felt dependent on secondhand contact with the outside world through their fathers, husbands and brothers, and a few took solace in addiction, whether alcohol, 'drowsy syrups' and pills, or 'that intensely feminine refreshment, shopping'. But by no means were all middle-class women stuck at home arranging flowers. Some chose a career, and throughout the nineteenth century, more and more women went into medicine, teaching, journalism and social work. White-collar work was increasingly professionalised during the second half of the nineteenth century, with previously lower-class professions, such as nursing, retail, office work and elementary school teaching, attracting middle-class workers. Women also began making forays into once exclusively male industries, for example printing, with feminists setting up the Victoria Press in 1860 and the Women's Printing Society sixteen years later. By 1915, of the 2,830 middle-class women in the Fabian Women's Group, 85 per cent were self-supporting and almost half were also supporting others.

There were more work opportunities for middle-class women as the nineteenth century progressed, with, for example, the Victoria Press (pictured) set up and run by women in the 1860s

Who Was 'Middle-Class'?

In 1801, around 475,000 people in Britain were said to be middle-class, but between 1803 and 1867, the middle classes expanded greatly. In 1851 this class was thought to contain a quarter of the population. But what did this actually mean? The Victorians perceived a wide gulf between upper working-class respectability and middle-class gentility, with women at the centre. The more ornamental and idle the women of a family were, the better the man of the house was seen to be providing for them.

As the middle classes expanded, the distinction between lower and upper middle-class women widened. The difference of a couple of hundred pounds a year had a huge social significance. A lower middle-class woman might scrape by on a hundred a year, cooking, cleaning and mending alongside one general servant, taking advice from one of Eliza Warren's bestselling household manuals, *How I Managed My House on £200 per Year* or *Comfort for Small Incomes*. But one upper-class woman recalled the endless leisure available to the women of her family in 1920s Liverpool, with 'three maids, a cook, a housemaid and a parlourmaid . . . gardener, chauffeur'. Her mother 'went into the kitchen to order the meals in the morning and that was it'. Many girls only lifted a finger to 'arrange a bowl of flowers occasionally'. Middle-class households usually had live-in servants. Perhaps just one maid, but having someone else to answer the door for them immediately placed the woman of the house as a 'lady'. 'Ladies' lived in leafier streets, in larger houses with more modern facilities, traditionally copying the upper classes by moving out of towns and cities into leafy suburbs, which also had the advantage of being cheaper. In 1848, the *Morning Herald* commented on the fashion for building and purchasing 'eligible family residences, desirable villas, and aristocratic cottages, which have nothing in the world of cottage about them except in the name'. Suburban garden cities were built, like Port Sunlight in 1905 and Hampstead Garden Suburb in 1907. When Isabella Mayson married Sam Beeton, he was expected to provide her with a house in the suburbs; her relations were horrified when Sam's business losses forced them to move to cheap inner-city accommodation.

Housing conditions improved dramatically throughout the nineteenth century for the wealthier middle classes. In the mid-1800s, there was piped water; in the 1850s, bathtubs; from the 1880s, indoor toilets. Oven ranges, washing machines, electric light and sewing machines were all in use by the early 1900s. Standards rose, and Eileen Whiteing, growing up in Edwardian London, defined herself as middle-class because she lived in a detached house, 'with four bedrooms, front and back hall, drawing-room, dining-room, kitchen, scullery, bathroom etc., plus a conservatory, aviary, tool-shed and outside lavatory for the gardener'.

Yet the lower middle classes often struggled to afford 'genteel' accommodation. In 1901, 'skilled mechanics; bank clerks; managing clerks; solicitors;

Images of the interior of a typical middle-class home

teachers . . . reporters . . . telegraphists; sanitary inspectors . . . police inspectors' earned around £150 to £200 a year in London. This could get them a 'snug little suburban six-roomed' house 'in one of the cheaper suburbs'. But a family on double or even triple that – 'the professional man, or the younger son with a narrow berth in the Civil Service' – was far more comfortable. Their wives would oversee the housework done by two or three servants, hire a governess for their daughters and dress fashionably. The upper middle classes aped the lifestyle of the upper classes, on a fraction of their resources: the large house, the servants, expensive dinner parties. The more affluent sent their sons, and later their daughters, to boarding schools and university.

Education

Middle-class girls learned the distinctions drawn between them and their brothers while they were still in the nursery. Parents aspired to send their sons to public school, yet daughters were seen as wives-in-training, with no need of algebra or Greek. Schooling was intended to prepare girls for 'a few years of life at home . . . days being filled by golf and tennis . . . some philanthropy . . . reading and perhaps a little art', before a 'suitable' marriage could be arranged for them. Helena Swanwick's memoir, *I Have Been Young*, recounts how, growing up in the 1880s, she 'could not help contrasting my condition with that of my three elder brothers, all at school and able to walk about freely in the daytime, while I was not allowed out alone and had to be content with some very poor piano lessons and a few desultory German lessons'.

Until well into the twentieth century, pupils at Girls' Public Day School Trust schools (founded in 1872) attended school only in the mornings to 'avoid strain'. Social commentators frequently argued that rigorous examinations and stress could affect girls' fertility. In 1923, a Board of Education report recommended that girls needed a slower pace, claiming that menstruation caused 'diminution of general mental efficiency'. Nevertheless, there were more academic options. The North London Collegiate School, founded by Frances Mary Buss in 1850, was the first independent girls' school in England. Frances Buss was determined to give her 1,000 students 'the best possible education at the lowest possible cost', providing them with a wider range of life opportunities.

Many middle-class girls, especially those in less well-off families, were taught at home, picking up scraps of knowledge from books and perhaps a few lessons from tutors. Elizabeth Sewell's autobiography tells how, in the early 1800s, she had 'English lessons at Miss Crooke's' and she also learned 'music and drawing' from 'very indifferent country masters', received French lessons 'from a very courteous old gentleman' and acquired 'a very little geometry in the holidays from our brother's tutor'. Her mother, the daughter of a clergyman, had educated herself from 'devour[ing] novels' and learning 'long passages from the great poets'. Some girls attended a day school, but these were not widespread until after the 1870 Education Act, when school boards took over, and built or expanded thousands of schools. Twenty-five years later, there were also about 15,000 private girls' schools in Britain. Boarding schools became more prevalent from the 1870s, but they were only available to the wealthier upper middle classes. In the 1830s, a fashionable boarding school might cost £500 a year, and the very cheapest around £30 – a large proportion of a lower middle-class income.

Girls' education, especially early in the 1800s, focused on decorative accomplishments, such as French, music, dancing, needlework and etiquette, and the quality of teaching at these schools was patchy. In the mid-1820s, 13-year-old Elizabeth Sewell found lessons substandard at her Bath school: 'The French master was an indifferent one . . . We had a second-rate dancing mistress, a fairly good sentimental singing master . . . a very inferior drawing master . . . and a music master with a great reputation and a violent temper.' Some middle-class parents were reluctant to send their daughters to school at all, fearing that they might encounter 'social inferiors'. Just before the First World War, the private girls' school that Katharine Chorley attended in Manchester only played games with three other local schools 'on secret grounds of social ineligibility'. In her memoir, *Manchester Made Them*, she recalled that the school games captain had to pretend that 'all Saturdays were regrettably filled until the end of term when a challenge was received from this or that establishment whose pupils were "not quite like ourselves".'

Governesses were a cheaper option, as one would do for several daughters, and they cost a fraction of boarding school fees during the Victorian era. The 1861 census shows that London fathers employing governesses were just as likely to be tradesmen, mariners and civil servants, as baronets and diplomats. Gwen Raverat, a Cambridge don's daughter had daily governesses. 'They were all kind, good, dull women,' she remembered in her memoir *Period Piece*, 'but even the most interesting lessons can be made incredibly stupid, when they are taught by people who are bored to death with them.' When they finished their education, most girls were expected to stay at home until they married, or perhaps forever if they remained single. In the 1910s, Katharine Chorley was dissatisfied with the stultifying 'life of a daughter at home' and wanted to go to Cambridge and find a 'proper job'. She was told that she was needed at home, to help her ailing father, 'taking down letters at his bedside and then spending long evenings alone by the fire in my own room'. Another woman recalled that in 1920s Liverpool: 'The odd one perhaps went into nursing or medicine, but not many of them had careers . . . usually they went to a domestic science school and did a year's course . . . it was quite unusual to go out and do a job.' But women were becoming more educated, and by 1929, 38 per cent of girls received a full secondary education and gained their Higher School Certificate. However, if they wanted to continue to university, girls had a far harder task than their brothers. In the

THE NEW WOMAN.

"You 're not leaving us, Jack? Tea will be here directly!"
"Oh, I 'm going for a Cup of Tea in the Servants' Hall. I can't get on without Female Society, you know!"

Punch *magazine satirises the 'new woman', the female intellectual, in 1895*

late 1870s, girls were 'coached for the same examinations as boys in half the time that boys had, and by women who were in many cases, themselves studying in their spare time for degrees, and who had no training of any sort as teachers'. Before the First World War there were few grants or scholarships; the majority involved a pledge to become a teacher after graduation. Without assistance, the fees were considerable. In 1899, Girton College, Cambridge, charged £35 and St Hugh's College, Oxford, £15, for board and tuition each term.

Those who got there found university a revelation. Helena Swanwick fell in love with 'intoxicating' Girton when she arrived in 1882:

> I had a study as well as a bedroom to myself . . . my own fire, my own desk, my own easy-chair and reading lamp . . . even my own kettle – I was speechless with delight . . . To have a study of my own and to be told that if I chose to put 'Engaged' on the door, no one would so much as knock was itself so great a privilege as to hinder me from sleep.

While female students had to endure being chaperoned to lectures there were compensations – a social life of 'debating, literary and philosophical societies, choral society'. The routine was roughly the same in most women's colleges:

The day began at 7:00am with a jug of hot water delivered to one's door . . . Prayers were at 8:00, followed by an informal breakfast and the reading of mail and the morning papers in the common room until 9:00 or 9:30, when all the bedrooms would have been cleaned . . . Some students had lectures in the morning, others were free to study. Lunch was designed to fit the different schedules . . . from noon to 2:00 or 3:00pm . . . Afternoons were spent on hockey, boating and long walks . . . from 5:00 to 7:00 . . . back to studying after their tea-break at 4:00. Dinner was at 6:00 or 7:00.

Many women students were also highly successful academically, like Philippa Fawcett, who was famously placed above the senior wrangler in the Cambridge mathematical tripos in 1890 – she could not be named senior wrangler herself because female students could not become full university members of Cambridge until 1948 and until 1919 at Oxford.

What Did They Do?

A boarding school training in 'accomplishments' provided little preparation for the monotonous routine of domestic married life, and there were few role models for different ways of living. Mid-Victorian girl, Mary Anne Hearn read magazines full of 'descriptive articles on men who had been poor boys and risen to be rich. Every month I hoped to find the story of a poor ignorant girl.' Most middle-class women were faced with two options: marriage and motherhood or a career. Suffragette Margaret Wynne was advised by her mother that, 'a bad husband is better than none'.

Spinsters over the age of 30 had little chance of marrying. A copy of *Reynold's News* from January 1908 included the following matrimonial adverts:

A superior person would like to marry an honourable man. Would make a capable farmer's wife. Aged 33.
Two friends (30, 32) highly respectable, domesticated, honourable women, would like to meet two friends or brothers, steady honourable men, retiring from navy or mechanics.

While upper middle-class women enjoyed the leisure provided by servants, less well-off middle-class women had washing, shopping, child-care, cooking, sewing and careful budgeting of expenses to contend with. In the 1890s, Helena Swanwick lived on her husband's academic salary of £250 a year, spending £30 on 'clothes and petty expenses, such as trams and postage and stationery and presents and the garden', but she had little left over for extras. Some women had to work, perhaps due to their father's business losses or the death or remarriage of a husband or parent. When

Emmeline Pankhurst's barrister husband died in 1898, she had five children to provide for. She moved the family to a smaller house and swapped her unpaid job as a Poor Law guardian for a salaried role as registrar of births and deaths.

Before 1860, there were few employment options for middle-class women beyond governessing and dressmaking. Later there were many more, but there was also increasing competition from the educated working classes for jobs in nursing, clerking, retail and teaching. Some positions were deliberately weighted towards middle-class applicants, restricted to those who could afford to take on poorly or even unpaid roles, and those requiring expensive training, such as librarianship and social work. There was a great deal of public opposition to women going out to work at all, especially middle-class women. It was seen as unfeminine – surely motherhood was a vocation enough, argued opponents like novelist Grant Allen, who wrote in 1895, 'A woman ought to be ashamed to say that she has no desire to become a wife and mother.' Well-off families were embarrassed by their female relatives working. Helena Swanwick's mother objected, 'Don't you see that I can't have her living in my house and earning her living like a man?' Looking back on her Edwardian childhood, Katharine Chorley concluded: 'A paid job for one of his womenfolk would have cast an unbearable reflection of incompetence upon the money-getting male.'

Not all women accepted these arguments. During the nineteenth century, 20 per cent of British firms were owned and operated by women. One married mother ran a button workshop in the early nineteenth century: 'She received the orders; made the purchases of materials; superintended the making of the goods; made out the accounts; and received money besides taking care of her growing family . . . She was an entirely self-acting, managing mistress.' Women opened shops, cafés, ran business training colleges and even cooking schools, as Margaret Fairclough did in the 1890s. There were thirty-eight female auctioneers in Britain by 1841. Women writers filled the shelves of the circulating libraries, and the most successful authors, like Maria Edgeworth, commanded up to £2,000 per novel. In the 1860s, Mary Elizabeth Braddon supported a large family on the proceeds of her thrilling, unfeminine, tales of murder, skullduggery and dangerous women.

Marriage and Motherhood

When they married, Victorian women were joined to their husbands financially, legally and physically. From then on, they had no separate identity: they could not give testimony in court without their husband's permission, and if they committed a crime in front of their husband, he was held responsible for failing to control his wife. Until the Married Women's Property Acts of the 1870s and 1880s allowed a woman to dispose of her own income, everything that she earned legally belonged to her husband. When Millicent

Much of a middle-class young lady's life was spent in leisure, and waiting for marriage

Garrett Fawcett had her purse stolen, she was humiliated to learn that the thief was charged with 'stealing from the person of Millicent Fawcett, a purse containing £1 18s 6d, the property of Henry Fawcett'.

This legal contract was binding. To gain a divorce in the late nineteenth century, women had to prove that their husband had behaved cruelly, deserted them, or committed bestiality, incest, rape, bigamy or sodomy. Divorce was expensive, and uncontested suits cost between £50 and £60; contested suits were up to £500. Between 1906 and 1910, there were just 638 divorces, and only 70 per cent of petitions were successful.

Some women rejected this fate, deliberately choosing to remain single – and free. Florence Nightingale wrote to her mother, in 1853: 'I have seen the husbands of my dearest friends curl their lips with a curious kind of smile at how little their wives understood them, & most men know their wives about as much as they know Abraham.' Others married for financial reasons. In the 1870s, Amy Pearce reluctantly married her cousin, who was over twenty-five years her senior. She ended two engagements to him in her early twenties, 'not feeling quite happy', and wishing desperately for 'someone I could respect very much' instead. She finally married her cousin when she was 33 and unlikely to receive another offer, her father's death also having left the family in poverty.

Once married, many women lived entirely separate lives from their husbands. While he went out to work, she was expected to run the household, and then be ready to provide 'comfort, inspiration and cleansing and rest' once he returned. Katharine Chorley recalled the complete segregation of the Edwardian inhabitants of Manchester suburb, Alderley Edge: 'After the 9.18 train had pulled out of the station, the Edge became exclusively female. You never saw a man . . . unless it were the doctor or the plumber, and you never saw a man in anyone's home except the gardener or the coachman.' Most newly-married women rapidly became mothers. In 1874, a study of over 50,000 middle-class women showed that 80 per cent gave birth within a year of marriage. Queen Victoria had nine children between 1841 and 1857, but she admitted to her eldest daughter after giving birth to her eighth child that she felt 'like a cow or a dog at such moments'. But a great deal of women, among them novelist Elizabeth Gaskell, felt that having children was one of the 'greatest & highest duties' of a woman's life. Elizabeth kept a diary in 1835, describing the childcare methods she used, not always successfully: 'Once or twice we have had grand cryings, which have been very distressing . . . I have sometimes cried almost as much as she has.' However, middle-class women started having fewer children from the 1870s onwards. In 1911, the birth-rate per 1,000 middle-class married men was 119, whereas for unskilled workmen it was 213. Women were learning about rather primitive methods of birth control to limit the size of their family. These were mostly unreliable: syringes, vaginal tubes, artificial sponges filled with quinine solution and rubber pessaries. Many wanted to avoid the health risks of multiple pregnancies, as five women in every 1,000 died in childbirth in the mid-1800s. There were severe gaps in Victorian gynaecological knowledge, and lack of hygiene was a huge killer. Many women, like Isabella Beeton, caught puerperal fever after being infected by doctors and midwives who did not wash their hands or clothes and transferred germs from other cases. Babies and children died in their thousands every year, and a multitude of diseases – measles, whooping cough, diarrhoea, smallpox and bronchitis – scythed down those who lived into childhood.

For some women, the experience of losing siblings or nephews and nieces drove them to a career in medicine. In the late eighteenth century, female surgeons such as Ellen Haythornthwaite, dentists such as 'Mrs De St Raymond' and bonesetter Sarah Mapp advertised their services in the newspapers. But in the early 1800s there were few hospitals outside London other than voluntary hospitals run by charities, and workhouse infirmaries. The Victorian period revolutionised medicine, and as the profession changed, so did women's opportunities within it. In the early 1800s, it was impossible for women to carve a career in medicine; yet by 1900, women like Shropshire nurse Agnes Gwendoline Hunt were able to make their mark in medicine. Hunt had been lamed by osteomyelitis as a child, but she was still determined to become a nurse and later opened the Shropshire Orthopaedic Hospital, the world's first open-air hospital for disabled people, in 1907.

Nursing

In the early 1800s, nursing was an unskilled working-class profession, but after the 1860s it began to attract 'ladies by birth and education . . . Daughters of clergymen, military and naval officers . . . doctors', as well as 'the upper servant class'. Over the Victorian period, nursing changed from virtual domestic service – scrubbing floors and applying poultices – to a profession. Nursing trainees, 'probationers', had to be over 23, single, equipped with excellent character references and able to pass the matron's scrutiny at interview. A few were 'lady probationers', who paid for their training and received easier conditions, but all probationers had to go through three years of rigorous training. Florence Nightingale's nursing training school at St Thomas's Hospital, expected a probationer 'to be fully taken up with her ward work, her necessary sleep and exercise . . . making and mending'.

While training, probationers lived in the hospital, and their daily routine was exhausting. In the 1860s, a nurse's day began around 6am:

> She has a breakfast of ham and eggs, coffee etc., and then enters the wards at 7. For about two hours in the morning both night and day nurses are on duty together, and the time is spent in sweeping the wards, washing the patients and preparing them for and serving them with their breakfasts. Between 9 and 10.30am, twenty minutes . . . to tidy themselves and take a lunch of bread and milk in summer or of soup in winter.
>
> After this they are on duty until about 1, when they go in two relays to dinner . . . Then follows a long spell in the wards, interrupted only by tea, taken usually in the wards, until 8.30 or 9.30, when . . . she goes off to supper of cold meat and vegetables. Finally she must be in bed with her light out by half-past ten.

Many middle-class girls gained their first sight of lower-class life on the wards. Frederick Treves recalled the customary inhabitants of the out-patients department at the Royal London Hospital, in 1867:

> a sniffing woman who had called for her dead husband's clothes; a breathless woman with a midwifry card, some minor accidents; a child who has swallowed a halfpenny; a serious casualty. On Saturday nights, the atmosphere is heavy with alcohol.

At Guy's Hospital, Emily MacManus was horrified by a fighting drunk, who, stark naked and writhing, was held down by nurses, 'roaring like a lion'.

Nurses who flourished might aspire to become matron, a powerful role within the hospital. Matrons organised the training of probationers and supervised all the other female hospital staff. Emily MacManus later wrote about her experiences as matron of Guy's Hospital, in the late 1920s. She managed a staff of 800 women, supervised the care of 700 patients, and organ-ised everything from laundry to pastoral care of nurses.

Female nurses also entered the battlefield. The Army Nursing Service, later Queen Alexandra's Imperial Military Nursing Service (QAIMNS), was formed in 1881 and, after 1884, women were employed in naval hospitals. In 1914, 2,000 nurses signed up for reserve and by 1919, there were 10,000 serving sisters. The women's First Aid Nursing Yeomanry (FANY), founded in 1907, was followed by the Voluntary Aid Detachments in 1909, who staffed

The Nurse — Old Style

Nursing became more professionalised, attracting more middle-class applicants from the mid-nineteenth century. These two cartoons compare the unqualified, slovenly nurse with her efficient, modern counterpart

The Nurse — New Style

hospitals at home and undertook unskilled duties – changing dressings, cooking and cleaning. During the First World War, various other women's nursing organisations appeared, such as the Women's Army Auxilary Corps (WAAC).

Like many of her contemporaries in the First World War, Emily MacManus went out to France as a civil nursing sister, and worked near Étaples, nursing 'convoys of broken men . . . dazed and exhausted by their grim experiences'. In 1918, she and her colleagues were tending to 3,000 men 'wounded on stretchers, on the grass, outside the huts'. 'Hell seemed very close,' she wrote in her memoir, *Matron of Guy's*. War work gained British nurses professional respect, and in 1916 the Royal College of Nursing was founded.

Doctors

Some women weren't satisfied with a nursing role. In 1859, Elizabeth Blackwell famously became the first woman in Britain to register as a doctor, after completing her qualifications in America. The General Medical Council moved quickly to stop other women from following suit and banned doctors holding foreign qualifications from registering. But, thanks to the efforts of hundreds of determined women such as Dr Elizabeth Garrett Anderson, Dr Frances Morgan Welsh and Dr Eliza Walker Dunbar, by 1901, 477 female doctors were on the medical register.

In 1869, the University of Edinburgh opened its doors to female medical students, and five years later, the London School of Medicine for Women was founded. Yet, once they gained their hard-won degrees, women doctors often struggled to gain employment. Most worked in women's and children's hospitals or for local authorities, but others founded their own hospitals and practices. In 1872, Frances Morgan and Elizabeth Garrett opened the New Hospital for Women in London; and Alice Moorhead and Emily Thomson began the Dundee Private Hospital for Women in 1896. Dr Jane Walker went further. In 1898, she bought two farms and used the land to found the East Anglian Sanatorium, the first female-run hospital treating male patients. Most female doctors did not earn large sums and some were subsidised by private incomes. Louisa Brandreth Aldrich-Blake, the first female master of surgery, worked at the New Hospital for Women, yet the bulk of her income came from land she had inherited.

Others used their qualifications to travel. After graduating from Queen Margaret College, Glasgow, in 1896, Elizabeth Ness Macbean Ross worked in the East End of London, but she was intrigued by an advertisement for 'a Lady Doctor for the East'. A month later she was travelling to Persia to become 'English doctor' to the Bakhtiari mountain tribe. Elizabeth embraced the new culture and was amused when some of the bibis (Bakhtiari women) offered her a place as one of their husbands' wives: 'I have had the hand of nearly all the Khans . . . offered to me in this way. I must say it is somewhat

*While still in her twenties, Elizabeth Ness Macbean Ross
worked as a doctor in Persia*

MAP OF BAKHTIARILAND

embarrassing when the gentleman himself happens to be present.' She had to deal with the occasional patient who claimed that a 'djin' had stolen his money, and many patients expected 'the European' to work magical cures. Sadly, Elizabeth died while working in a Serbian fever hospital during the First World War.

Teachers and Governesses

During the first half of the nineteenth century, female teachers and governesses did not need qualifications. Many impoverished gentlewomen became governesses, and there were far more impecunious young ladies than teaching vacancies. The 1861 census reveals that there were 24,700 governesses in England and Wales. These women earned very little, most between £35 and £80 a year from 1830 to 1890. As well as earning a servant-sized salary, governesses had to put up with being 'higher class' than their fellow servants in the household, but never the social equal of their employers. In 1858, a woman journalist wrote scathingly:

> Just let a remote idea be entertained of marriage between a son, or any other member of the family, and the governess; why, another siege of Troy would scarcely occasion more commotion – the anger, scorn, vituperation lavished on the artful creature.

However, while working for a 'particularly attentive and affectionate' widower, 19-year-old May Pinhorn was surprised when 'He got me into a summer house and told me he hoped I would be his wife, an offer I promptly and brutally refused.' Some women preferred the independence of setting up their own schools. Mary Carpenter ran a Bristol ragged school in the 1840s, and Amy Pearce and her sister set up a school in the 1880s, but these ventures were financially precarious. There were some success stories, like that of Mary Smith. Born in Oxfordshire in 1822 to a shoemaker and a cook, Mary raised herself from a mother's help to establish a girls' school. While caring for the children of a local wealthy Quaker family, she was allowed to use their library, and taught herself French, German and Italian. When she died in 1889 Mary left nearly £1,500 in her will. While earlier governesses managed with more humble skills, by the mid-nineteenth century they were expected to teach far more: grammar, history, geography, French and perhaps Italian or German, as well as ornamental skills like sewing, music and painting. In the 1840s, measures were taken to professionalise governesses and teachers. Queen's College was founded in 1848, and special lectures were held for governesses on useful educational topics, from theology to ancient history, and 'instruction in the art of teaching'. There were free evening classes on the same subjects for 'governesses who are employed during the day'. Teacher training institutions sprang up all over the country, like Cheltenham Ladies

A GENERIC DIFFERENCE.

First Schoolgirl (Sweet Eighteen). " I AM SO TIRED OF WALKING ALONG BY TWOS AND TWOS IN THIS WAY ! IT 'S AS BAD AS THE ANIMALS GOING INTO THE ARK ! "

Second Ditto (ditto ditto). " WORSE ! HALF OF *THEM* WERE MASCULINE ! "

Thousands of impoverished middle-class women turned to teaching and governessing in the Victorian era, not always with happy results

NO SINECURE.

Proud Mother (to the new Governess). " AND HERE IS A PENCIL, MISS GREEN, AND A NOTE-BOOK IN WHICH I WISH YOU TO WRITE DOWN ALL THE CLEVER OR REMARKABLE THINGS THE DEAR CHILDREN MAY SAY DURING YOUR WALK."

College, founded in 1853, and the Maria Grey Training College, founded in 1878.

Women teachers also formed support networks through organisations such as the Teachers' Guild of Great Britain, the Association of Headmistresses and the London Schoolmistresses' Association. The Countess of Cardigan recalled that governesses in aristocratic families 'had their own "set" and they formed a sort of society in society . . . cheerful, smiling young women who seemed thoroughly to enjoy themselves, and who did not long for a small smothered life in the shape of marriage with a parson'.

With the increasing number of girls' day schools after the 1870 Education Act, more elementary teachers were required. By 1914, the number of female elementary teachers had increased by over 800 per cent, since 1875. Traditionally, these women came from the lower middle class. Elementary teachers stayed on at school and learned to teach as 'pupil teachers'. After the 1902 Education Act there were scholarships to allow poor but able girls to attend state secondary schools and teacher training colleges. These were much needed, as the average cost of a university education was around £400 in 1911.

Once a teacher had gained her coveted first post, she had to adapt to regimented school life. Most day school teachers taught from 9am to 12pm, then 2pm to 4.30pm, and completed preparation and marking in the evenings. In 1894, Miss Harris, a head teacher at the Ben Jonson School, considered that a new teacher was often lonely 'perhaps living in lodgings, isolated beings far from home and friends'.

Teachers were accountable to parents and local authorities – the school board inspectors, as well as the headmistress. Mary Eliza Porter, one of the first graduates of Queen's College, was full of enthusiasm to instil in her charges the precept that 'knowledge was a good thing'. But, as headmistress of the Bedford Girls' Modern School in 1882, she found the interference of the school governors frustrating. They blocked her attempts to improve the school curriculum and refused her request to allow the cleverest girls to stay on until 18. Grammar school and university teachers were upper middle-class university-trained women, but as more and more women chose to teach, jobs became more in demand. The most popular career option for female university graduates at the turn of the century was teaching. Starting salaries declined as the profession became overcrowded: in 1860, new secondary school teachers earned between £120 and £220, but by 1890 just £70 to £80 was on offer. Governesses, too, faced dwindling employment prospects. In 1861, two-thirds of governesses were under 30, and the peak of the profession was around 35 – older women were seen as less energetic and were paid lower wages. For most, retirement was a bleak prospect unless they had savings or some inheritance to live on. Each year the Governesses' Benevolent Institution supplied a handful of women with much-needed annuities, but ex-governesses were still to be found in workhouses and institutions all over the country. As in most professions, the First World War changed things for female teachers. They took over male teachers' jobs in boys' schools for the first time. The Frœbel Educational Institute newsletter for 1916 proudly mentions a Miss Marin who 'took the place of a man in a boy's school for the period of the war', in Tyneside. By the Second World War, female teachers still earned around 20 per cent less than their male counterparts and even the most highly qualified female academics at universities were often scraping by on a fraction of male colleagues' wages.

Many teachers left their job when they married. In London around 10 per cent of female teachers were married in 1911, but only 4 to 5 per cent elsewhere. Mrs Robb, a domestic science teacher, saw teaching as a way to pass

Typing was embraced by women, as seen in this Punch *cartoon from 1876*

MR. PUNCH'S ILLUSTRATIONS TO THE POETS.

" So careful of the Type, she seems."—*Tennyson.*

the time before marriage. She would meet friends to go shopping after work: 'We were all engaged, looking at the engagement rings, looking at the furniture that we might want.' In the early 1900s, retired teachers might receive money from the Teachers' Annuity fund, contributed to by working teachers, and a state pension after 65, but the two together were not more than £40 or £45 a year.

Office Work

In the first half of the nineteenth century, offices were exclusively masculine, but from the 1870s female clerical workers were taken on. In the 1851 census, nineteen women were listed as commercial clerks; by 1891 there were 17,859. Commercial activity rocketed during the mid-Victorian period, creating larger companies and larger mounds of paperwork. New technology – telegraphs, typewriters, adding machines, card indexes and telephones – as well as the penny post system and postal orders required extra workers.

Most of this was rather dull work. Women were given the dead-end jobs and repetitive tasks like shorthand and typing. They were expected to assist their bosses selflessly, not to aspire to replace them. 'The successful secretary flings herself with zest into her employer's affairs, whatever they may be, enjoying, as it were, a vicarious career,' wrote W Mostyn Bird, in *Woman at Work* in 1911. But women embraced office work, and between 1861 and 1911

THE CENTRAL TELEGRAPH OFFICE: INSTRUMENT GALLERY.

Women workers in the Central Telegraph Office in 1870

94

there were 500 female clerical workers for every man in a similar role. At the turn of the century, 562,000 women worked in the Civil Service, one of the largest employers of women along with local government and the General Post Office. More professional roles in banking, law and railway companies remained male preserves.

Business training colleges, often run by women, opened up to train middle-class young ladies with means – albeit slender ones in many cases. In the 1890s, Miss Cecil Gradwell and Miss Richardson ran a 'school of business training for gentlewomen' in Westminster. For twelve guineas their students could acquire 'shorthand, typewriting and bookkeeping' and attend 'lectures on practical secretarial work'.

Once they gained an office job, women had a hard battle to achieve promotion, let alone equal pay. In 1871, the Post Office considered that the 'wages, which will draw male operators, but from an inferior class will draw female operators from a superior class'. At the Prudential insurance company, male clerks could receive salaries of up to £350, whereas, in 1891, only seventeen lady clerks made over £60. Extra training could raise wages: in 1910, typists could earn from £1 a week, but those with shorthand and one language might get £4. Sidney Webb wrote in 1891, 'For women's work the "gentility" of the occupation is still accepted as part payment.' Most clerical jobs required women to put up with segregated offices, to dress smartly on low wages and to live with their parents or in dingy lodgings. Even so, these jobs were highly sought after.

Once women employees married, they usually had to leave work. The marriage bar concealed the fact that there was little chance of promotion anyway. Even large employers of women, like the Civil Service, excluded them from senior roles. In 1912, the Royal Commission on the Civil Service concluded that 'in power of sustained work, in continuity of service, and in adaptability to varying service conditions, the advantage lies with men'. There was open opposition to women working in offices. One letter in the *Liverpool Echo* in 1911 advised 'intrepid "typewriter pounders"' who 'gloat over love novels or do fancy crocheting during the time they are not "pounding"' to:

fill in their spare time washing out the offices, and dusting same . . . [which] would give them a little practise and insight into the work they will be called upon to do should they . . . marry one of the poor male clerks whose living they are doing the utmost to take out of his hands.

By 1911, women made up just 6 per cent of the higher professions, and only 8 per cent in 1951.

Lady Clerk. "Yes, they actually complained in the office to-day because we were talking too much. They wouldn't do that if we were men!"

Women increasingly worked in offices, although these were often segregated. However, not everyone was happy with this state of affairs

Social Work

Throughout the nineteenth century, there was a strong ethos of giving, promoted by Queen Victoria and upper-class women such as Angela Burdett Coutts, who personally donated over one million pounds to charity. Ever eager to copy their social superiors, the middle classes followed suit. In 1885, the total of all charitable donations given in London was larger than Sweden's national budget. As well as giving money, many middle-class women also undertook charity work. By 1857, 'There was not a town in the kingdom that did not have its lying-in society, female school, visiting association, nursing institute, and many other charitable organisations.' And these were largely run by women.

While the most popular charitable causes were vulnerable groups like women and children and the elderly, women got involved with all aspects of society. Some middle-class women struggled to relate to lower-class life. Teacher Mary Smith was surprised when her evening classes for young working women on 'childcare, thrift, cleanliness, and cheerfulness' failed to attract large audiences. Some societies were less practical than others, like the Pure Literature Society, the House-Boy Brigade and the wordy Ladies' Association for the Benefit of Gentlewomen of Good Family, Reduced in Fortune Below the State of Comfort to which They Have Been Accustomed. Many middle-class women were also involved in fund-raising activities: subscriptions, charity balls, bazaars and 'fancy fairs' selling ornaments and pieces of sewing. Others worked more directly with those they wanted to help. The Ladies' Sanitary Association, established in 1857, aimed to 'popularize sanitary knowledge by writing and distributing simple and interesting tracts on sanitary and domestic subjects'. One popular form of social work was visiting the poor, in the style of the country gentlewoman calling on her husband's tenants. Visiting societies and committees provided food, blankets and coal. Most 'lady visitors' visited weekly and took notes on what they found. Katharine Chorley recalled her mother's visiting routine in the early 1900s:

> Mother would 'go visiting' in Manchester . . . looking up the housewives of Ancoats from an accredited list . . . listening to the tale of their difficulties, giving sympathy and advice and arranging for material help . . . but if it were done in a prying and patronising spirit, and sometimes it was, then it became the most revolting insult.

Some women chose to visit with charitable organisations, others worked in their local area independently, and a few even founded their own charities. Octavia Hill was passionate about improving working-class housing, so she bought housing blocks, renovated them and rented them out to poor families. By 1912, Octavia owned over 2,000 properties; all with playgrounds, workshops, savings clubs and gardens. Lady visitors took to visiting prostitutes and when entering brothels were instructed 'to wear elegant clothes, clean gloves and a pleasing hat so that prostitutes could see that virtue was not always dowdy'. But most undertook less controversial work. In 1862, Anna Sewell founded a Band of Hope Temperance Group in Abson-cum-Wick village, tempting children with 'capital cake and bread and butter'. She and her mother also taught a working men's club of forty, on 'any subject likely to awaken interest and inquiry, such as geography, natural history, biography . . . science'. Helena Swanwick ran a working girls' club, organising plays with dancing and singing in Edwardian Manchester. In the late Victorian era more women were elected to local government positions than today. Miss Martha Merrington became the first female Poor Law guardian for Kensington in 1875. Female guardians were given scintillating 'feminine' jobs such as supervising female scrubbers and washers, but many did real good, and, by 1910, there were 1,655 of them. Women also sat on school boards from the 1870s, including Londoner Helen Taylor, who campaigned for school fees to be abolished.

Suffragettes

The women's suffrage campaign was a largely middle-class movement. It had its beginnings in the 1860s, with the Kensington Society, a group of suffragists who lobbied Parliament and handed out pamphlets, without much effect. The movement became more visible when Millicent Fawcett set out to combine disparate women's suffrage organisations in 1897, starting the National Union of Women's Suffrage Societies (NUWSS). This was followed by the Women's Social and Political Union (WSPU), founded in 1903 by Emmeline Pankhurst.

The WSPU included women from all walks of life – shop assistant Jessie Spink campaigned alongside Mary Home, daughter of an Indian Army officer. But their tactics steadily became more violent, and members began to commit acts of vandalism – breaking windows, burning buildings, slashing paintings, even firing cannons, as well as demonstrating in the streets. On 18 November 1910, when another bill proposing to extend voting rights to women was voted down, there were violent demonstrations in Parliament Square. During that day, which was later dubbed 'Black Friday', 115 women were arrested, and others were treated brutally by the police, who beat, kicked and groped them.

By 1913, the NUWSS had distanced itself from the WSPU's militant tactics. That year, the Temporary Discharge Act (known as the 'Cat and Mouse Act') was introduced to avoid suffragettes on hunger strike dying in prison and becoming martyrs to the cause. The women on hunger strike were released and later arrested again once they recovered. Although the Qualification of Women Act had allowed women to sit on councils and be elected as mayors in 1907, women were not granted the vote until 1918. Six million British women over 30 and the wives of male householders were finally able to vote then, although Lord Curzon and many other critics still proclaimed that female voters would be the downfall of the British Empire. Women finally gained the vote on equal terms with men in 1928.

How Did They Live?

Leisure

'Oh, weary days – Oh evenings that never seem to end – for how many years have I watched that drawing room clock and thought it would never reach the ten,' Florence Nightingale wrote of her youth. 'Women's business,' as Sarah Stephens put it her novel, *Passages From the Life of a Daughter at Home*,

Middle-class courting couples were permitted a little more freedom than their upper-class counterparts, as imagined in this illustration from Once a Week *(16 July 1864)*

in 1845, was 'to find something to "pass" the time . . . in drawing or in music or literature or worsted work . . . reading aloud.' *Every Girl's Book* (1860) lists uninspiring entertainments open to young middle-class girls: spillikins, fancy work, embroidery, silk work, making wax flowers. For older women there were card games, bridge and sewing.

Just before the First World War, Katharine Chorley observed that the housewives in the Manchester suburb where she lived 'filled in time' paying calls, 'an accepted social duty', taking up at least a couple of afternoons a week. If no one was at home, three cards had to be left, 'one of her own and two of her husband's; her card is left for the mistress of the house, and her husband's for both master and mistress'. If they were in, then she still had to 'leave two of her husband's cards on the hall-table, and neither put them in the card-basket nor leave them on the drawing-room table, nor offer them to her hostess, all of which would be very incorrect'. The slightest slip in etiquette 'showed ignorance of polite manners, and therefore brought the caller's whole social position into question'.

Bored young women devoured romantic novels: the Edwardian best-sellers, Baroness Orczy's *The Scarlet Pimpernel* and De Vere Stacpoole's *The Blue Lagoon*. The market for women's magazines rocketed in the second half of the nineteenth century. *The Englishwoman's Domestic Magazine* was first published in 1852, and family periodical *The Family Friend* distributed nearly five million copies in ten years during the 1840s and 1850s.

Other middle-class ladies enjoyed active pursuits; ice-skating, gardening and cycling from the mid-1890s. Helena Swanwick 'scoured the Cheshire and Derbyshire lanes within a radius of twenty miles' with her husband at week-ends. Playing games was 'a regular occupation . . . the tennis club courts would be dotted with white long-skirted figures hitting balls with a serious zeal'. Many middle-class women supervised elaborate dinner parties, and those with fewer servants would also have cooked the food. Assisted by just one servant, Helena Swanwick prepared supper parties for eight, with menus like 'Asparagus soup, Oyster Patties, Pigeon Pie, Pineapple Jelly, Cheese Straws', or 'Oyster Soup, Stewed Ox-tongue . . . picked walnuts, Cheese Souffle, Meringues'. Dinners began with soups – 'consommé' or 'purée' – then two kinds of fish, two or three 'entrées of sweetbreads, partridge cutlets'; then meat courses, one of poultry, another of roast meat; a mixture of savoury and sweet dishes, completed by an 'ice', water or ice cream and fruit. A well-stocked cellar was essential; the author of one dinner party manual advised allocating half a bottle of champagne to each man and a third to a lady, as well as a 'sound dinner claret'. Dances and balls were the main events of most young girls' lives. At the end of the nineteenth century, Helena Swanwick's family gave dances at home: 'The carpet was taken up and the floor re-stained and polished with beeswax and turpentine . . . deco-rated the fireplaces and marble mantel-pieces with flowers stuck into banks of moss,' and hung the garden with Chinese lanterns. Helena recalled:

100

When the paid musicians had been dismissed, my father would play for us as long as we had legs to move; we drew the curtains and danced to dawn in, and finally . . . we had a scratch breakfast of consommé and remnants of food and coffee, some of the party going off for a plunge in the Serpentine.

Larger balls were imposing affairs lit with 'a positive blaze of light' from chandeliers, and extra candles suspended from the ceiling, Chinese lanterns and coloured lamps. There were floral decorations of clustered evergreens and foliage, and exotic cut flowers. There would be a piano player, or at grander occasions an orchestra would be hired. Refreshments were served – a full supper of cold chicken, salmon, game pie, sandwiches 'of potted game, chicken, or lobster', jelly and 'light French confectionery'. Lots of wine, champagne and brandy, and mineral water and soda water for the abstemious.

Health

Eating all this stodgy food, Victorian women were predictably worried about their weight. Health issues were surprisingly similar to those debated by women today. They fretted over their complexions, weight and mental health. One 1840s manual complained:

Witness our easily excited feelings, witness our late hours of rising, our sofas and easy chairs, our useless days and dissipated nights . . . our pallid faces . . . our over-fed and over expanded forms, enfeebled by indolence, and suffering the worst species of debility – the debility of fat.

Quack drugs and panaceas were aimed at gullible middle-class women with plenty of disposable income – 'Morrison's Pill' taken with lemonade, the 'Harness World Famous Electropathic Belts' and 'Pink Pills for Pale People' were just a few. But for all their drugs, solutions and powders, their warmer, more spacious and cleaner homes, middle-class women were often little healthier than working-class housewives. The largest cause of death for nine-teenth-century women was respiratory problems, acquired through spending days inside poorly ventilated rooms with closed, heavily curtained windows and constantly burning coal fires.

Dress

Women were also preoccupied by fashion, which changed hugely during the nineteenth century – from the flimsy muslins of the 1800s to the vivid colours, thicker skirts, braids, frills and tassels of the 1830s, and the more fitted 1870s

Middle-class women were keen to adopt whatever the aristocracy was wearing, even impractical crinolines in the 1850s

creations designed to show off the waist. In the 1890s, women wore skirts that 'came right down to the ground and Sunday dresses had to have little trains behind . . . heavy tweed "walking skirts", which kept on catching between the knees . . . [and] swept the roads'. Women's magazines carried advertisements for cosmetics, corsets, skin tonics, hair dyes – 'the New Parisian Vaporizer, or Beethan's Glyceran and Cucumber Lotion' – into suburban homes. In the cities quacks such as the notorious Madame Rachel fleeced wealthy clients for lotions and potions promising eternal youth.

Even less well-off girls, like impoverished draper's daughter Anna Sewell, managed to enjoy fashion in the late 1830s. She wrote to her mother: 'I am going next time we go to town to get a black merino frock which I think is necessary because it will soon be too cold for prints in the morning so I shall have to take my mousline de laine & it would never do to take my black silk for the afternoon.'

Twenty-year-old Amy Pearce from Gloucester noted down her latest outfits in her diary, during 1873:

My best dress is a soft drabby grey trimmed with satin to match, a long plain skirt & pretty polonaise. Then I have a circular cape of black cashmere trimmed with black silk and yarn lace, & a straw bonnet trimmed with black velvet and white ribbon with a tip of ostrich feathers. I am going to have two white muslins for every day & I have a black and white silk & a pretty golden grey shot silk. My every day hat is a turn down black and white straw trimmed with black velvet ribbon.

In 1822, writing to Fanny Keats, Hampstead fashion-lover Fanny Brawne sighed, 'I really think over economy the most expensive thing there is.' The two girls discussed their new outfits: 'Margaret and I are red hot to make a chinks gown apiece. Mine is to be a la Jacke,' and detail dressmaking tips: 'the bands of course will be put in with small cords covered with muslin . . . I think net sleeves out of the question.' Girls were rigged out in complicated layers of clothing. At school in the 1880s, one young girl wore a sweltering array of clothes:

Thick, long-legged, long-sleeved woollen combinations
Over them white cotton combinations, with plenty of buttons and frills
Very serious, bony, grey stays with suspenders
Black woollen stockings
White cotton drawers
White cotton petticoat-bodice
Rather short, white flannel, petticoat
Long alpaca petticoat
Pink flannel blouse
High starched, white collar
Navy-blue tie
Blue skirt, touching the ground
Leather belt, very tight
High button boots.

In her memoir, *Period Piece*, Gwen Raverat described how she despised constricting fashions:

Except for the most small-waisted, naturally dumb-bell-shaped females, the ladies never seemed at ease . . . For their dresses were always made too tight . . . their stays showed in a sharp ledge across the middles of their backs. And in spite of whalebone they were apt to bulge below the waist in front.

In the early 1890s, a writer on etiquette advised that morning dress 'should be simple and refined, and suited to the time of day . . . a white embroidered dress . . . coloured cotton'. Dinner dresses were supposed to be 'silks and satins, velvets and brocades . . . trimmed with lace', with the neck and arms 'generally covered'. In the ballroom, women wore light fabrics of 'silk, tulle, net, gauze . . . trimmed with lace and flowers. The bodice . . . low, with short sleeves; or cut open in front and at the back, with shoulder straps, and sleeves to the elbow', with artificial flowers.

Underneath, corsets were 'absolutely necessary', especially for stouter women. Underwear was 'gracefully cut' and of 'white linen or cambric', because a 'virtuous woman has a repugnance to excessive luxury in her under-clothing'. Coloured cotton stockings were worn in summer, with boots; or stockings fastened with suspenders. Over the top, women wore a chemise, drawers under a petticoat, and a slip bodice, which were all supposed to match.

Changes

Like their Edwardian and Victorian predecessors, middle-class women today still try to balance the demands of a family with a life outside the home, gain equal pay with male colleagues and get ahead in the professions. Until 1910, no women worked in banking, and at the outset of the First World War there were no female barristers, diplomats or judges. When Janet Young married in 1935 while working for the Bank of England – an employer with a firm marriage bar – she had to keep her husband secret, marrying again, 'officially', in 1938. The marriage bar was not formally dropped in most professions until after the Second World War. Many women also had to sacrifice the chance of a family to pursue careers. In the early 1900s, only 22 per cent of female social workers in Birmingham married and those who did married nine years later than average.

Gradually middle-class women workers became more accepted; in 1906, working women had their own magazine, the *Working Gentlewoman's Journal*. More and more went, in larger numbers, to school, to university, and the office. In 1931, single women made up 51 per cent of the workforce over 35. Cecily Hamilton, observing the platform of a London railway station as the morning trains arrived from the suburbs, during the 1930s, wrote, in *The Englishwoman*, in 1940:

> a veritable torrent of humanity pouring past the barriers and out into the streets; there to disperse to its daily labours in office and warehouse and shop. And that torrent will be largely composed of women; working women of all degrees, from the teashop waitress and the dressmaker's assistant to the manager of a flourishing business.

Women banded together and created their own support networks. Vera Brittain set up fee-paying baby clubs in the 1920s, and a group of single working women formed the Over Thirty Association, in 1935. By the Second World War, women were finally living Victorian spinster Geraldine Jewsbury's dream of 'better days, when women will have genuine, normal life of their own to lead'.

Researching Middle-Class Women

- **Female graduates**: Many universities and colleges have archives with material on female students, consisting of records, photographs and, in some cases, material donated later in life. This is particularly true of Oxford and Cambridge colleges: for example, former women's colleges such as St Hilda's in Oxford has a college archive and a detailed list of its holdings available on the college website. If you are researching a graduate of an Oxford or Cambridge college, then check the college website and contact their archive or library. Other universities also have collections of records on early women students, although holdings and dates do vary. For example, the John Rylands Library at Manchester University has material dating from 1851: calendars, reports, matriculation and attendance registers; examination records and papers; university newspapers and magazines; photographs of students, staff, buildings and events.

- **Magazines:** Many magazines aimed specifically at middle-class women were launched in the Victorian era, and dipping into these can give a sense of the period, and women's aspirations and beliefs at the time. Some of the most popular include: the *Englishwoman's Domestic Magazine* (1859–72), *Home Notes* (1894–1937), *The People's Friend* (1869–present) and more aspirational titles such as *The Lady* (1879–present) and *The Queen* (1862–1970 – incorporated with *Harper's Bazaar*).

  Anthologies such as *Victorian Women's Magazines*, edited by Margaret Beetham and Kay Boardman (Manchester University Press, 2001) give an overview of the culture of women's magazines during the period. For a more academic approach, try Margaret Beetham's *A Magazine of her Own?: Domesticity and Desire in the Woman's Magazine, 1800–1914* (Routledge, 1996). The British Library has extensive holdings of magazines, but you might also find copies at university libraries and large city libraries. There are also plenty of digitised copies on Google Books (http://books.google.com).

- **Parish newsletters:** The parish church was often a focal point for charitable activities such as mothers' unions, bazaars, and Sunday schools – all of which were well-attended by middle-class women. Their records can be found in local libraries and record offices.

- **Sources for suffragettes:** Before you start researching a suffragette, visiting the Museum of London is worthwhile as it has an enormous collection of material on the women's suffrage movement. It has a large display of banners, photographs and even the inedible bread ration doled out to one suffragette in prison.

  The two main suffrage periodicals were *Votes for Women* (the WSPU publication) and *The Common Cause* (the NUWSS publication). Some of the best places to find these are Manchester Central Library (Elliot House,

Deansgate, Manchester M3 3WD; 01612 341900), which has a suffragette fellowship collection, and the Women's Library in London (London Metropolitan University, 25 Old Castle Street, London E1 7NT; 020 7320 2222; www.londonmet.ac.uk/thewomenslibrary).

The National Archives holds a range of records on suffragettes, mainly in the Cabinet Office holdings (series CAB 41), with detailed reports and correspondence on the issue. Other documents include complaint letters from prisoners (series HO 45) and data gathered by the Metropolitan Police on suffragettes (series MEP 02).

- **Sources for office workers:** The Women's Library has records of many national women's organisations such as the Association of Women Clerks and Secretaries (1920–36) and the National Association of Women Civil Servants (1901–59). It is worth checking local archives for local or regional organisations. Many of these organisations also published newsletters and reports, like *The Woman Clerk*, published by the Union of Women Clerks and Secretaries (1925–31).

Sources for teachers

School records: Many schools, especially long-running or private institutions, may have preserved their records. Others will have passed them to local archives, or, if you are unlucky, they may have been destroyed. Start by checking local archives and the school, if it still exists. But if you can't find anything, then don't worry – there are plenty of other sources to try. Check commercial directories to find former locations of schools which have since closed down.

The Girls' School Year Book: This is the reference book for the Association of Headmistresses, which lists staff, qualifications, curricula and fees of private schools. The records of the Association of Headmistresses are held at Warwick University.

Parliamentary reports: There were many reports on education during the nineteenth century, resulting in lots of material for researchers, although this is often unwieldy. Michael Argles has written a useful guide to parliamentary reports on education, *British Government Publications in Education in the Nineteenth Century* (History of Education Society, 1982). Full reports are accessible at the British Library and larger city and university libraries. Examples include: the 1816 Report of the Education of the Lower Orders of the Metropolis; the 1834 Report on the State of Education; the 1861 Royal Commission on the State of Pauper Education in England; the 1867–8 Report of the Schools Inquiry Commission; and the 1870 Report of the Census on Education.

School board reports, log books and minutes (LEA reports after 1902): These were undertaken after the 1870 Education Act, and are often very detailed, with information on salaries, purchases, attendance figures, truancy and parent complaints. You can find them in local and county record offices.

Charitable institutions: Many ex-teachers and governesses had to turn to charity when they were no longer able to work. Their archives may contain letters, lists of pensions and even specific cases. For example, the Governesses' Benevolent Institution, based in London (archives held at the London Metropolitan Archives). Search the National Register of Archives for specific charities (www.nationalarchives.gov.uk/nra).

Sources for doctors and nurses

The General Medical Council: The GMC will conduct a search, for a fee, to find details of the registration of any named doctor (Regent's Place, 350 Euston Road, London NW1 3JN; www.gmc-uk.org).

Archives: London Metropolitan Archives have the archives of various early hospitals founded by women and employing female doctors, for example the New Hospital for Women and the Annie McCall Maternity Hospital (London Metropolitan Archives, 40 Northampton Road, London EC1R 0HB). Some archives are held by existing hospitals, like the Archive of the London School of Medicine for Women, which is held at the Royal Free Hospital Archives (7 Lyndhurst Gardens, London NW3 5NU; www.royalfreearchives.org.uk).

The Hospital Records database contains over 3,000 entries and can point you to where the archives for specific hospitals are located (www.nationalarchives .gov.uk/hospitalrecords).

The Englishwoman's Year Book: This was published annually by Adam & Charles Black between 1875 and 1916 and contains details of all female doctors listed, at first by date of their qualification, and later on by location. Some of these have been digitised and are freely available online, but you can find a complete set at the British Library.

- **Sources for military nurses:** Female non-combatants received the same campaign medals as male soldiers. You can find them in the *London Gazette,* which is searchable online at www.gazettes-online.co.uk. Search the Commonwealth War Graves Commission website for details of women killed on active service (at www.cwgc.org.uk).

  The National Archives should be your first stop for researching military nurses. Its holdings are outlined in an excellent research guide (available online at http://tinyurl.com/39su78m) and archives including the register of the Royal Red Cross awarded to nurses.

  The Army Medical Services Museum is also worth a visit to pick up valuable background information (Army Medical Services Museum, Keogh Barracks, Ash Vale, Aldershot GU12 5RQ; www.ams-museum.org.uk/museum).

Chapter 5

ARISTOCRATIC WOMEN

'Ladies were ladies in those days,' wrote Gwen Raverat, looking back on her 1890s youth in *Period Piece*, 'they did not do things themselves, they told other people what to do and how to do it.' At the end of the nineteenth century, thousands of British women 'had never made a pot of tea . . . been out in the dark alone . . . travelled by train without a maid . . . or sewn on a button'.

The elite were a minority – consistently less than 1 per cent of Britain's population, and never over 5 per cent. While the aristocracy was geographically widespread, 'society' was a claustrophobic 'large family' where everyone knew each other and intermarried. Some found this intimidating, as did Mary, Countess of Minto, who confided to her journal in 1851 that she felt 'utter unfitness for the position I was called to fill'.

Their proximity to power and wealth made upper-class women automatically significant in a way that lower-class women could never be. Lady Dorothy Nevill proclaimed that an aristocratic woman 'elects without voting, governs without law, and decides without appeal'. Elite women used their position to achieve political influence, get involved with philanthropy and the arts, or simply to have a good time.

They were also highly visible and vulnerable to criticism, especially within their closed world of rigid standards. A genuine 'lady' possessed a core of 'sterling, moral worthiness', the *Alexandra* magazine explained to readers, in 1864. She would 'never try, by any means, to appear other than she really is', Lady Colin Campbell wrote piously, in her book on etiquette. Yet Lady Colin's own infamous divorce had long excluded her from Society. Those who fell short of the ideal were shunned by their peers, often with very little cause. When widowed Lady Charlotte Guest married her children's tutor she was cut, but women were criticised for much more minor deviations. In 1835, Lady Powlett compared bourgeois Lady Shelley to 'a very disagreeable instructed [sic] Governess, whose vulgarity annihilates one'.

Who Was an Aristocrat?

'Nobles' were traditionally either *nobiles majores* (the peerage: dukes, marquesses, earls, viscounts, barons) or *nobiles minores* (gentry and baronets).

An English country house party in 1855

Women only bore courtesy titles belonging to their husband or father. As the Victorian period progressed, there were fewer landowning families, and more men acquired fortunes and titles through industry and trade. During the era, between 400 and 500 different noble families had representatives in the House of Lords, but in 1870, 900 families had an income of over £10,000.

The greatest social distinction was financial. Many aristocratic families owned huge swathes of land. In 1873, over three-quarters of the land in Britain was owned by 7,000 people, (0.5 per cent of the population). And about 6,000 families owned estates of between 1,000 and 10,000 acres (providing an income of £1,000 to £10,000 a year). Another 750 owned 10,000 to 30,000 acres, and at the pinnacle 250 possessed over 30,000 acres and £30,000 a year.

In 1901, the *Cornhill Magazine* published examples of living costs for Londoners on certain incomes. Those with £1,800 a year in 1901 were placed as upper middle-class, with a modest house and up to four servants, but those on £10,000 could afford a London mansion with 'ten or twelve servants and a really good cook'. However, only those who followed the Season, making the rounds of country house parties, could really consider themselves among the elite.

Education

Life for most upper-class Victorian children consisted of nannies and the nursery, perhaps meeting their parents formally once a day. 'I can never remember being bathed by my mother or even having my hair brushed by her,' recalled Gwen Raverat. 'We did not feel it was her place to do such things.' Small gender differences slowly crept into the nursery. While their brothers played noisy games outside, girls had deportment lessons; while boys were sent to boarding school, aristocratic girls were taught by governesses, their mothers and sometimes masters for certain subjects. After the First World War, upper-class girls began attending boarding schools, but during the Victorian era this was anathema. When 14-year-old Mildred Hugh Smith mixed with middle-class pupils at Kensington High School in the 1880s, it was considered 'revolutionary'.

Molly Bell, the daughter of a millionaire iron manufacturer, felt 'bored to death all the time':

> My mother's idea of the equipment required for her two daughters was that we should be turned out as good wives . . . able to take our part in the social life of our kind . . . mathematics, political economy, Greek and Latin – there was no need for any of these. No girl that we knew was ever trained for any career or profession.

Governesses were of varying quality and could exercise a great deal of power over their charges. Seven-year-old Lucy Caroline Lyttelton was terrorised by hers in the 1840s: 'I used to be taken out walking on the parade with my hands tied behind me, terrified out of my wits . . . continually put between the doors and often whipped.' Later in life, Lucy Caroline campaigned to improve education for girls.

Frances Power Cobbe's memoir describes her mixed procession of governesses in the 1830s, starting with:

> a good creature properly entitled 'Miss Daly', but called by my profane brothers, 'the Daily Nuisance'. After her came a real governess, the daughter of a bankrupt Liverpool merchant, who made my life a burden with her strict discipline and her 'I-have-seen-better-days' airs . . . a remarkable woman, a Mdle. Montriou, a person of considerable character.

At 14, Frances was sent to finishing school in Brighton, hundreds of miles away from her home in Ireland. She hated the 'din of our large double school-rooms . . . four pianos might be heard going at once . . . there were girls reading aloud to the governesses'. The room always had several miscreants, in full evening dress, being punished, 'with their faces to the wall; half of them being quite of marriageable age'.

Upper-class girls commonly completed their education by the age of 17 or 18. However, towards the end of the nineteenth century, a small but steadily growing number attended university. Louisa Lumsden, bored with the social round, went to Hitchin, the forerunner to Girton College, Cambridge. Helen Gladstone went to Newnham College as a 28-year-old spinster, and found student life 'a refreshing change from the aimlessness of most girls' lives'.

What Did They Do and How Did They Live?

Débutante

'I consider it every girl's duty to marry £80,000 a year,' Alice Catherine Miles confided to her diary, in 1868, aged 17. Her view was not unusual – upper-class girls entered society as débutantes for one reason: to be married off. 'Marriage must inevitably remain the chief end and object of the Gentlewoman,' advised Lady Violet Greville in *The Gentlewoman in Society*. And there was no time to lose: 'A woman's brightest beauty lasts only ten years – from twenty to thirty . . . Like a far-seeing general she marshals her forces, counts the cost, and proceeds bravely on the skirmish through the hot oppressive mazes of the London ballroom.' In 1860, just one in sixteen spinsters married after turning 30.

A débutante's 'coming out' began with her presentation to the monarch at the start of the 'Season'. Queen Victoria held drawing rooms where débutantes, dressed according to strict palace rules, were presented in the early afternoon, their carriages lining the road to Buckingham Palace. Early Victorian débutantes were almost exclusively the daughters of peers, but by

While in London for the Season, most aristocrats lived in large town houses, with armies of servants, like these in Berkeley Square (left) and Chelsea (right)

the 1860s, the daughters of wealthy merchants, bankers, and financiers were also presented. *The Queen* magazine protested snobbishly that: 'The wives of all Members of Parliament are presented and they, in turn, present the wives and daughters of local squires and other small magnates. There is no knowing where this may stop.'

Wealthier families gave their daughters 'coming out' balls:

> The girl, smiling . . . looking fresh and innocent enough in her white toilette holding the bouquet of lilies of the valley . . . is introduced to so many new people, who come streaming up the staircase . . . Presently she is led out to the dance, like a lamb to the slaughter.

The Countess of Cardigan attended her first fancy dress ball as a virginal 'Louis XV shepherdess', in 1842. 'Mama took endless pains,' she remembered in *My Recollections*. 'My hair was exquisitely poudré, and my beautiful pink

Most aristocratic girls became débutantes and were presented to the monarch, then launched in Society and expected to find a suitable husband

Balls were lavish affairs and extremely intimidating for new débutantes

and white gown, garlanded with roses.' Some 'debs' found the process intimidating. Lucy Caroline Lyttelton went to her first ball 'with the highest expectations of pleasure', only to find herself being 'dragged into the first quadrille of 32' and mercilessly 'quizzed and pitied'. It was also tiring – Dorothy Nevill in *My Own Times* recounted how she went to fifty balls, sixty parties, thirty dinners and twenty-five breakfasts in her first season, and Alice Miles was treated for exhaustion.

Flirtation alone involved a great deal of concentration. William Tayler, a London footman to the aristocracy observed in his diary:

> It's amusing to see the young ladies, how they manoeuvre to make the gentlemen take notice of them. They will loose their pocket handkerchiefs or drop their gloves, that the gents may offer to find them . . . The girls are up to hundreds of these little manoeuvres at parties to induce the men to begin talking to them.

The Season followed the parliamentary recess of Easter to August and consisted of races, river parties, regattas, picnics; continuing in the autumn with country house parties and shooting. A typical débutante's routine involved rising late, an informal lunch, then a chaperoned afternoon stroll, a game of tennis or a ride. Afternoons were spent paying or receiving calls and exchanging a 'naughty story or fie-fie anecdote', the latest scandal or fashion. Dinner was the big event of the day, with elaborate dress. Alice Miles often took two hours to dress for dinner. After dinner, the ladies retired to the drawing room briefly, leaving the men to smoke cigars, and would then either remain at home, perhaps playing card games, listening to musical performances and conversing, or they might go out to a concert, sometimes followed by a ball, which could last until dawn.

Food for the aristocracy was as much about display as sustenance. Throughout the nineteenth century, the idle rich scheduled their days around meals. During the Season, breakfast might be as late as 10am, then luncheon – more a meal for the ladies – followed a few hours later by tea – 'genuine French coffee, strawberries and cream, peaches, grapes, cakes, and all sorts of other little delicacies' – around 5pm, a multiple-course dinner at 8 or 9pm, then supper in the early hours, if they attended a ball, of luxurious 'chicken pâté de fois gras, jellies and fruit'.

Until the First World War, aristocratic dinners consisted of: a 'good deal of meat . . . several entrées, two soups, two fishes, two sweets, and a savoury, only half of which any reasonable person can possibly wish to partake of'. In her gourmet cookery column in the *Pall Mall Gazette*, Elizabeth Robins-Pennell criticised excess at dinner parties: 'Dish follows dish, conceit is piled upon conceit; and with what result? Before dinner is half over, palates are jaded . . . every new course awakens fear of the morrow's indigestion.' Even a simple dinner for two, like one enjoyed by the newly-wed Cecilia Ridley in

Débutantes about to hit the Season in the 1870s are satirised

1841, involved a mountain of food: 'a small wee bit of lamb' for her husband, a whiting each, a roast partridge for her, with roast potatoes, then pudding, cheese, and a 'sumptuous dessert – grapes, brandy cherries, cakes, French plums'. All this over-indulgence created many corpulent, florid-faced gentlemen, and the ladies fared just as badly. Nathaniel Hawthorne described Victorian middle-aged British women as 'composed of sirloins, and with broad and thick steaks on their immense rears'.

When she wasn't scoffing mountains of food, a débutante spent a great deal of time dressing, making several costume changes a day – perhaps a morning dress, a riding outfit, a dress for afternoon calls and a dinner and ball gown. For Edwardian women, a 'different dinner gown was considered essential for each evening, a weekend in the country could not be undertaken without a mountain of clothes'. Dolly Davy worked as a lady's maid to an 18-year-old débutante in the early 1900s; she recalled in *A Sense of Adventure*: 'She was very fussy; she bathed, oh perhaps five, six times a day . . . I'd have to wait there for her coming out, and see that her clothes were done.' During the early twentieth century, fashions became more experimental, and designers 'hobbled the acquiescent English women in harem skirts, hung them with fox furs, draped them in pearls, and enveloped them in wired tunics and jewel-laden capes'. Elaborate hairstyles were constructed with false hair, padding and wire frames. At a typical country house dinner in 1868 Alice Miles wore 'a cloud of white tarlatane, wings of the same on my shoulders, festooned and trimmed everywhere with trailing ivy sprigs, interspersed with clusters of scarlet rose-berries'.

Successful debs, like Alice, reached almost celebrity status, and 'had paragraphs respecting my fair face and beautiful toilette inserted in more newspapers than I should care to count'. She enjoyed listing 'the handsome young millionaires I have at my feet', but rarely took them seriously. 'He was so struck dumb with admiration that he could not even bring out a compliment,' she laughed about one. 'An occasional "Oh my God" was the only vent it found in words.' Underneath her bravado, the need to make a good marriage was paramount. At her first ball, Alice's cousin advised her:

Before introducing anyone Augustus gave me a rapidly whispered enumeration of their possessions and social standing: for instance –'Beauty Campbell, Captain, Guards, splendid place in the North, £20,000 a year.'

– Captain Campbell – Miss Miles.

It was very difficult not to laugh with the individual standing unconsciously opposite you.

Alice considered suitors in strictly commercial terms:

Sir Samuel has tried to inveigle me into a flirtation, but as I had previously ascertained he has only £4,000 a year . . . there would be no interested side in any proceedings and he is not sufficiently good looking to render interesting, and a flirtation devoid of either of these indispensible elements does not at all enter into my plan of action.

She recorded without criticism her friend Edith Wood's engagement to 'an old Essex bumpkin between 45 and 50, owner of a fine unencumbered property and £12,000 a year . . . she

Full evening dress at Edward VII's court, pictured in the Pall Mall Magazine

unblushingly asserted that she'd marry the Devil himself, if he'd £10,000 a year.' Most upper-class families wanted their daughters to marry only within the 'correct' class. At 23, Lady Eileen Elliot fell in love with a man deemed unsuitable by her family, and she took refuge in 'sleeping draughts and stimulants . . . burgundy at luncheon and dinner'. The consequences for those daring enough to elope were severe, often resulting in exclusion from family fortune and society. Evelyn Stanhope gossiped about a Miss Osborne who had eloped in 1874, 'the Osbornes are so irrevocably angry . . . Mrs O has entirely cut her out, settled the estate on the Duchess of St Albans.' Considered equally unsuitable were marriages between young grooms and older brides, on the grounds that the wife's childbearing years were limited. Lady Louisa Antrim remarked in 1901, 'Victoria Lothian *married* Bertram Talbot last week – it is beyond words – revolting I think – she 59 – he 37! – 22 years between them.' Some saw through the frills and champagne to the commercial transaction beneath: 'the vanity and weariness of it all . . . its hollowness and insincerity'. Alice Miles knew that, as she lacked a large dowry, most of the men she flirted with might admire her looks, but would never propose. A few women enjoyed a more romantic courtship. In 1872, 20-year-old Emily Jowitt from Leeds wrote excitedly to a friend that when she found herself alone with Squire Dearman Birchall on the way back from church, 'just as we were going down the carriage drive, he proposed . . . the suddenness of it all took my breath away'. While engaged, Emily remarked that she and Dearman 'generally spooned a good deal and said "Oh my darling I do love you so"'.

Marriage

After a deb had caught her man, they would usually marry after an engagement of between a month and a couple of years. In the 1890s, a wedding ceremony might involve: 'a choral service, soldiers to line the church if the bridegroom be in the army, a bevy of bridesmaids, with a page clad in antique garb . . . an atmosphere of flowers and champagne, bride-cake and orange blossoms.' Upper-class marriages were excessively elaborate occasions. When Lucy Caroline Lyttelton married at Westminster Abbey, she was followed down the aisle by twelve bridesmaids.

Directly after the wedding, and perhaps a short honeymoon or European travels, married life began: 'The husband returns to his military duties, his House of Commons, or his club life, while the lady chooses a bosom friend to run in couples with her, to share her opera-box, her pony carriage, her walks and rides, her party at Ascot, and her expeditions on the river.' Marriage could be a struggle after the repressive conventions surrounding courtship. When Mary Hardcastle was proposed to by Robert Collier in 1873, she had 'literally only beheld Bob twice in morning costume [i.e. not at a party]'. Footman William Tayler saw upper-class marriage in black-and-white terms: 'If a gentleman marries a lady, it's for her money, and in a short time he gets tired of her, and takes up with a kept girl again, and treats his wife like a dog.' Barbara Leigh Bodicon argued that a married woman's existence was 'entirely absorbed in that of her husband . . . A woman's body belongs to her husband . . . and he may enforce his right by a writ of habeas corpus.' Some took this literally. Constance Ward's husband made her 'put on all her jewels for his special benefit when they were alone. He would admire her thus for hours.' After she died in childbirth, he displayed her corpse to a friend. Opening her mouth, he remarked, 'I always told you she had bad teeth.' Until 1928, wives promised to 'obey and serve' their husbands in the Anglican marriage service. This was often taken literally. Queen Victoria advised her newly-married daughter: 'Let it be your study and your object to make his life and his home a peaceful and happy one and to be of use to him and be a comfort to him in every possible way.' Lady Cecil Talbot's father told her:

Young ladies in the mid-Victorian era, like this one pictured in 1860, were expected to marry and bear children. Having a career was unthinkable for the majority

'After the Almighty, let your husband reign in your heart. You now have no duty, but to obey him. Watch his looks and fulfil all his wishes, conform yourself to his habits and inclinations.' While women were to obey, their husbands had made no such promise, and it was conventional for them to have mistresses. In her teens, forbidden to attend the theatre one evening, the Countess of Cardigan sneaked in anyway. 'I peeped out from the curtains of the box . . . directly opposite to me there sat papa and the General, with two very pretty women.' Newly-married aristocratic women, especially those in landowning families, were under pressure to produce a male heir, and preferably a couple of spares. Aristocrats had large families: Lady Elizabeth Holland (died 1845) had fifteen pregnancies and ten children; Sarah Sophia, Countess of Jersey (died 1867) had ten pregnancies and eight children, and Frances Anne, Marchioness of Londonderry (died 1865) had ten pregnancies and seven children. Miscarriages were common and in 1894 a GP estimated that 80 per cent of women suffered at least one. Pregnant upper-class women carried on with the social round, exercising 'only a little more than ordinary care'. With most women enduring several pregnancies, most were pragmatic. Mrs Graham Smith wrote to a friend, in 1883, 'I am so well, just as well as any other person and as active as a cat . . . I expect to have a very easy time, and shall be alright again directly.'

Later in the century, with better access to birth control, elite women had fewer children. *Burke's Peerage* shows that during the 1840s the aristocracy gave birth to an average of seven children; in the 1850s and 1860s they produced six; but, in the 1870s, just four; and during the 1880s, three. Not all pregnancies were welcome. Pregnant for the twelfth time, Lady Henrietta Stanley wrote to tell her husband, who protested, 'What can you have been doing to account for so juvenile a proceeding?' She replied, 'A hot bath, a tremendous walk and a great dose have succeeded but it is a warning.'

While far fewer Victorian women were unfaithful – or had the opportunity to be – some, trapped in unhappy marriages, grasped any chance of love. Débutante Alice Miles married at 18 in 1870. Her new husband, George Duppa, was thirty-three years her senior, but his large fortune somewhat cancelled out this defect. A few years later, Alice began an affair with dashing Major Gerald Ames and had at least one child by him while still married. Duppa soon became suspicious. 'I gradually dropped her,' he wrote to his lawyer. 'I never kissed her or took her into dinner . . . we continued to have meals together. I did not do anything to set the servants speculating.' Avoiding a scandal was also essential for Alice, as a cousin of the infamous Lady Colin Campbell. In 1887, with Duppa threatening divorce, she attempted suicide. But Duppa died before the divorce case could reach court and become public. Alice was able to marry Ames a respectable year later, with her reputation unstained.

Until 1857, divorce was only available by Act of Parliament, and by this date only four women had gained one. The 1857 Matrimonial Causes Act made divorce slightly easier to obtain, setting up a new divorce court and granting maintenance to divorced women. Divorce was, however, no less scandalous. Alice Miles's cousin, Lady Gertrude Colin Campbell created the gossip of the season, in 1885, when she and her husband both filed petitions for divorce. Five years earlier, at the age of 23, Gertrude Blood had become engaged to Lord Colin Campbell, after three days' acquaintance. Their marriage was delayed by the Campbell family's disapproval and his poor health – he neglected to tell his fiancée that he had syphilis. In 1883, Lady Colin was granted a judicial separation on grounds of cruelty, that Lord Colin had knowingly infected her with syphilis.

Two years later the Campbells were back in court, this time seeking a full divorce. Lady Colin gave infidelity and cruelty as grounds, while Lord Colin claimed that Lady Colin had had liaisons with the head of the London Fire Brigade, his doctor and a general. The case was extensively reported in the papers, with salacious anecdotes. There were plenty of them: for instance, the jury visited the Colin Campbells' former home to check whether it was

Divorce was to be avoided at all costs during the Victorian period, but increasing legislation made it easier for couples to separate. Some saw this as the breaking down of society. In 1891, the Illustrated Police News *asked its readers, 'Is marriage a failure?'*

possible for a servant to have seen Lady Colin and a lover in the throes of passion through a keyhole. Lady Colin was described as possessing 'the unbridled lust of a Messalina and the indelicate readiness of a common harlot'. The divorce was never granted, as neither side could conclusively prove adultery.

Lady of the Manor

A mistress was integral to the running of a large country house. If the male owner was unmarried his mother or single sister usually took on the role. A few women inherited their own estates, like Lady Londonderry, who managed her husband's estates after his death. Some, like Jane Austen's Lady Catherine de Burgh, had the gift of a living at their disposal and terrorised their clergymen. 'I had an opportunity of saying I liked short sermons & quick service & I advised the leaving out of the Litany,' wrote Lady Constance Stanley of hers. Even before the 1882 Married Women's Property Act, increasing numbers of upper-class women ventured into estate business: Georgina Somerset raised livestock; Augusta, Countess of Dartmouth, kept poultry; and Anne Athole managed herds of cows.

Many women lived full-time in the country, visiting London during the Season. In smaller establishments, the mistress might act as her own house-keeper, but bigger country estates were filled with staff, visitors and extended family. Unlike her middle-class counterpart, the mistress of the house came into contact with dozens of people during the day. Frances Power Cobbe ran her elderly parents' country house:

> I went every morning regularly to my housekeeper's room and wrote out a careful menu for the upstairs and downstairs meals. I visited the larders and the fine old kitchen frequently, and paid the servants' wages on every quarter day; and once a day went over my lists of everything in the charge of either the men or women servants.

The lady of the house might also furnish, decorate or design the gardens. Lady Dorothy Nevill oversaw the construction of exotic gardens at Dangstein in Hampshire. The mistress was also a figurehead, organising and presiding over social events for staff, tenants' parties, local charity work and drumming up votes for relatives at election time. In *The Gentlewoman in Society*, Violet Greville described how the country gentlewoman was seen as a leader in society:

> Her words, her manner, her dress, her opinions are eagerly canvassed and quoted by the neighbours; her bonnets and hats are copied by the wives and daughters . . . Not a bazaar can be organised without her patronage and aid; not a charitable committee held, not a church

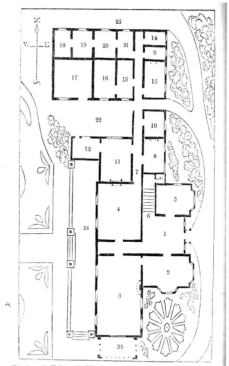

Fig. 1. — 1, Hall. 2, Morning room and library. 3, Drawingroom.
4, Dining-room. 5, Gentlemen's business room. 6, Staircase.
7, Passages to offices. 8, Housekeeper's room and store closet. 9, Old
store closet. 10, Butler's pantry. 11, Kitchen. 12, Scullery.
13, Servants' hall. 14, Dressing-room for men-servants. 15, Dry larder,
or pantry. 16, Wet larder and salting-room. 17, Laundry. 18, Cheese
room. 19, Scullery and churning-room. 20, Butter room. 21, Dairy.
22, Kitchen court. 23, Road to stable. 24, Terrace. 25, Conservatory.

*A typical manor house in the 1840s,
as imagined in* A Lady's Country
Companion *by Mrs J. Loudon*

restored, nor a lawn tennis party voted really successful, unless it be graced with her presence.

On a visit to one of her estates, Kirkstall Abbey near Leeds, the Countess of Cardigan was greeted with great pomp: 'A salute of fifteen guns was fired when we arrived in a carriage drawn by four horses, which some of my tenants took out and drew the carriage themselves to the Abbey, where I gave a great dinner to three hundred of my Yorkshire tenantry.' Country gentle-women also found plenty of time for amusements. They hosted house parties with hunting and shooting or games of archery, battledore and shuttlecock. Lucy Caroline Lyttelton enjoyed a 'paper hunt' in 1862: 'I never went such a dance: over two miles across country, of which a mile was mostly running; and though I skirted many fences, there was plenty of modest scrambling.' Far from London and 'civilisation', some were bored. When German nobleman Hermann Pückler-Muskau toured England in the 1820s, he found country house parties turgid occasions. One evening at Cobham:

Five ladies and gentlemen were very attentively reading in various sorts of books . . . another had been playing for a quarter of an hour with a long-suffering dog; two old members of Parliament were disputing violently about the Corn Bill; and the rest of the company were in a dimly-lit room adjoining, where a pretty girl was playing on the piano-forte, and another with a most perforating voice, singing ballads.

The Lady's Country Companion advised women to take interest in small things:

When you first begin to walk out, you will probably find the beauty of the scenery quite sufficient to interest you; but after a time, as your walks must all necessarily partake of the same character you will want a little variety, and you must make sources of interest . . . you see a mole-hill with a mole caught and hanging in a trap . . . a rather small bird with a dead mouse in its beak . . . a bit of stone that appears composed of various particles.

Country squire's daughter Linda Birchall kept a diary in the late 1890s that reflects the monotony of some country women's lives:

Jan 1st. This morning Violet and I went to church, and apart from Canon Scobell, were the only congregation. We bicycled to Gloucester after-wards . . . Went to Watsons and were photographed . . . Parish Tea this evening, coming back about 10.15.
    Jan 13th Violet and I shopped in Gloucester . . . Jack, Violet and I went a drive with the ponies

Jan 15th We had a Band of Hope [temperance organisation] treat in the Reading Room. It went off well, prize-giving, games and tea . . .

Jan 16th I took a Sunday school class . . .

Jan 21st We have had a very melancholy day. Percy went back to Oxford this morning.

Linda later travelled in Germany, but it was thought too exciting for her and a doctor advised 'no riding, biking, dancing, practising, dinner parties, concerts, theatres, in fact nothing except three walks a day' for a whole year.

A Career?

Aristocratic women were meant to marry, not to work. Although until the Married Women's Property Act of 1870 everything a wife owned legally belonged to her husband, relations often established settlements or trusts for wealthy women when they married. Cecilia Ridley had a yearly income of £300 after she married in 1841.

As Frances Power Cobbe found out, an aristocratic upbringing did not insulate women from financial insecurity. When her father died, Frances was left a trifling £200 a year (she was used to £130 pin money) and had to leave her home, which her brother had inherited. She had to 'make over to my brother my private possessions of ponies and carriage'. Frances felt helpless, 'I cut off half my hair, being totally unable to grapple with the whole without a maid.'

Most elite women never needed to work. Instructed in a little painting, singing and sewing, they were at best dilettantes. Violet Greville described lady amateurs: 'Women in Society write music, like Lady Hill Arthur and Lady Radnor; they even compose operas and operatorios, like Miss Ellicot; they paint admirable pictures, like the late Lady Waterford and Mrs HM Stanley,' but none of them engaged with her hobby in a professional way.

Others turned to society. In 1881, Emily Birchall was triumphant when her 'At Home' was attended by over 100 people, including Oscar Wilde. Writing to her mother, she described proceedings:

We were very busy preparing; the flowers took me the whole mortal morning, till 1.40, then arranging the room and superintending the florists doing up the plants in the conservatory . . . We had a great spread of fruit, about 20 dishes of strawberries, peaches, greengages, raspberries, gooseberries, nectarines, currants . . . cakes, tea and ices and claret and champagne cup . . . People dribbled in and then came a rush . . . there was quite a babel of talk between the music.

The Edwardian era was a sporting golden age, and women became 'lady-cyclists, lady-cricketers, ladies who shoot, and ride, and fish and do

125

As an Irish aristocrat, Frances Power Cobbe enjoyed a privileged upbringing in a beautiful country house, but when her brother inherited everything on her father's death, Frances was forced to try to earn a living

everything that men can do', even 'pistol-shooting or archery, or rifle shooting at a target'. Less active young women occupied themselves with books. Frances Power Cobbe spent her days on 'Astronomy, Architecture, Heraldry'. Alice Catherine Miles published essays in *Vanity Fair* under a male pseudonym, but refused to write professionally: 'What is money and a name to a woman when compared to her fortune? To make a book really interesting you must describe daring passions no man would care that his wife should have experienced.' Less well-off women took up aristocratic shopkeeping, as 'lady dressmakers' or florists, exploiting their connections. Others found it harder to earn a living. Frances Power Cobbe supplemented her small income by 'trudging three times a week for seven years to an office in the purlieus of the Strand to write articles for a halfpenny newspaper'. Not all were constrained by social expectations; Eveline, Lady Portsmouth, continued to teach after her marriage in the 1870s. A few gained unique independence through their work, like Lady Colin Campbell, who enjoyed a successful career as a journalist, author and painter. She became an art critic for the *London World*, the editor of the *Ladies' Field* and exhibited her paintings several times.

Politics

While women were unable to pursue their own political careers, many meddled in the careers of male relatives and influenced events. Before 1832, when legislation explicitly banned women from voting, a few landowning single women and widows actually voted or used male proxy voters. As property owners or friends and relatives of candidates, elite women were uniquely close to power and used their connections to help – and sometimes to meddle. Women's involvement might have been satirised as 'petticoat politics', but it could be effective. Upper-class women wrote letters, gave dinners, canvassed voters for male relatives standing in elections and wheedled patronage from influential friends.

In 1868, Mrs E.H. Bruton wrote to each of her tenants: 'SIR – I request you will vote for my father, J.W.S. Erle-Drax, Esq., on receipt of this.' Lady Louisa Sandwich was an active campaigner from the early 1800s. From the 1870s onwards, Lady Derby, Lady Salisbury, Lady Randolph Churchill and Louisa Athole were all politically active. Countess Louisa von Alten was married successively to two Conservative politicians – the dukes of Manchester and Devonshire – and became a leader in the Conservative world herself in the 1860s.

Others acted as political hostesses. Lady Holland and Lady Jersey gave small political dinner parties in the first half of the 1800s and there were dozens throughout the nineteenth century – for the Whigs, Lady Holland, Lady Palmerston and Lady Waldegrave; for the Tories, Lady Jersey, Lady Dorothy Nevill and Lady Londonderry. Lady Warwick described these salons:

Entertainment among the elite was undoubtedly an art. The enchantment lay in setting us at ease in a luxury that was exquisite, without thought of cost. Here, in an atmosphere of beauty, men and women reposed . . . matters of high importance to the State were constantly decided between Liberals and Conservatives in the country houses of England.

During the 1880s, women's party organisations such as the Conservative Primrose League and Women's Liberal Federation were founded. The Primrose League had a 'Ladies' Grand Council', whose members – including Clementine Churchill, Duchess of Newcastle and the Countess of Jersey – worked alongside men. A few aristocratic women became suffragettes. Lady Constance Lytton was 39 when she became a militant suffragette. She called herself 'one of that numerous gang of upper-class, leisured-class spinsters, unemployed, unpropertied, unendowed, uneducated . . . economically dependent entirely upon others', but was determined to be useful to others. Constance threw a stone at a politician's car radiator and was imprisoned, but released due to ill health. Undeterred, she dressed in ragged clothes and posed as an impoverished seamstress, being arrested once more. Sadly, the effects of forcible feeding made her into an invalid for the rest of her life.

Philanthropy

Philanthropy was a central role for elite women, especially for those in the country. *The Lady's Country Companion* advised gentlewomen, in 1845:

As your husband is the last descendant of an ancient family, it is particularly incumbent upon him, and, of course, also upon you, to keep up as much as possible the kindly feeling which existed in olden time between the lords of the soil and its cultivators . . . you should occasionally walk through the village . . . call frequently on your poorer neighbours . . . with the ostensible appearance of employing them in some little work . . . make enquiries into what your poor neighbours have for dinner . . . get the daughters taught the best way of cooking food suitable to their rank in life.

Elite women often struggled to identify with the lower classes. Lady Monkswell criticised Irish peasants: 'We passed 20 or 30 wretched cabins, & the untidy hair & the ragged petticoats of the women & girls that looked out entered into my soul. It costs nothing to comb your hair or to cut the rags off the bottom of your petticoat.' Lady Westmoreland wrote snobbishly of a tenants' ball in 1858: 'Not only do the wives and daughters of the good people wear hoops, big sleeves . . . but they dance the polka, *schottische*, and quadrilles . . . It makes one die of laughter to see them.'

Country gentlewomen organised the distribution of leftover food and old clothes for cottagers. Linda Birchall packed Christmas boxes of 'tea, coffee, sugar, bacon, tobacco, cocoa, chocolate, currants, raisins, apples, oranges, and crackers'. Eveline Portsmouth allocated whole days to visiting the poor in 1871: 'Called on the Roberts, visited the Almshouses left 2/ a piece for the old Women – Called upon the Corvans, the Heeneys & Hardens, Corcorans, Flynns, Mahoneys . . . left 4/ for the beggars.' They also visited ill tenants or paid for medical care. Alice Duppa (née Miles) records in her diary for 1875: 'Read to Mrs Jenner, gave her a rabbit. Poor old dear, she is always so grateful for the small mercies in the shape of my august presence. To Mrs Atkins I gave the lovely quilt I made last night as she had the most awful cough.' Not all upper-class women made such gestures, but a large proportion did some form of charity work. Before the 1880s, few took part in organised charity work, which was dominated by the middle classes. The urban elite were more likely to raise money than sit on committees, taking on less involved tasks, like Lady Colin Campbell, who sang at benefit concerts, and Harriet Sutherland, who lent her house for anti-slavery meetings. Money-making bazaars, concerts and garden parties were all pleasant, conscience-salving ways of 'helping' the poor without dirtying delicate aristocratic hands. Catherine Gladstone held bazaars, garden parties and fancy sales in the early 1800s. These were often highly successful, and in 1872 a bazaar at the Convalescent Hospital in Blackrock, Brighton made over £1,000.

Upper-class women made donations to charitable causes. One year, Harriet Sutherland donated to: clothing clubs on the Staffordshire estate, the British Ladies' Society for the Reformation of Female Prisoners (one guinea), Brompton Hospital for Consumption and Diseases of the Chest (three guineas) and the School of Discipline, Chelsea (two guineas). But not all had access to much ready cash. In 1840, Harriet Sutherland had to turn down an anti-slavery campaigner:

> You know no Woman has much to give, those that would seem to have more, the Wives of large proprietors have always many claims, for with means never very large, the Poor are considered particularly their own, & I have many to take care of in England & more in Scotland.

Upper-class women also had strong links to educational charities. Their involvement varied from 'financing schools, selecting teachers, and daily management, to holding classes, to the provision of, and occasional presence at, an annual treat'. Lady Charlotte Guest set up a women's night school in 1848, while Henrietta Stanley, (later Lady Eddisbury) visited poor families to persuade mothers to pay to educate their children.

When heiress Louisa Twining started visiting the poor in the 1840s her eyes were opened to the life of the poor: 'I learned as much as to character and the amount of depravity in our midst as I knew little before.' Many like Louisa devoted themselves to charitable work which had a practical and lasting effect: Lady Jeune set up a charitable home for poor women, Lady Breadalbane assisted orphanages, and Lady Tweedsdale organised 'happy evenings for poor children'. Lady Grey Egerton and Lady Selkirk organised the rather less effective-sounding Gordon League: 'a Sunday society for cheering and ennobling the lives of the people by music.'

Changing Fortunes

During the 1870s, many upper-class families, especially the landed gentry, fell into financial difficulties. Poor grain harvests, combined with cheap imported American grain, lowered agricultural income and land values. When death duties were introduced in 1894 – rising from 15 per cent in 1909 to 60 per cent by 1939 – large estates began to be broken up as aristocrats sold off big chunks

Women's clubs, like the Lyceum (pictured) became very popular during the late Victorian period, as women gained more freedom

of land. The First World War resulted in a wave of dead upper-class young men, and yet more death duties to be paid. By 1910, the industrial income of England was three times greater than the agricultural income, and wealthy manufacturers' daughters made their débuts at court alongside aristocratic young ladies. The 1914 edition of *Burke's Peerage* listed half the number of families that had appeared in the 1863 edition.

In 1892, Lady Greville concluded *The Gentlewoman in Society* with the view that society was crumbling: 'The modern lady sees her empire slipping from her . . . giving place to a kind of democratic equality.' Edwardian women had greater freedom than their forebears. 'Bachelors of the fair sex' went to women's clubs – over twenty existed in London alone – such as the Ladies' Army & Navy in Cork Street, the Empress in Dover Street and the University Women's Club in Audley Square. 'Everyone is doing the same old thing – just flirting and dining and dancing,' wrote Mary Curzon to a friend about 'Society', in 1910.

There was a sense that Victorian formalities were dead and gone, and in any case, fewer people were able to afford to dedicate themselves solely to Society. More and more men and women took on politics, charity work – and even careers. In 1934, Lord Esher proclaimed:

> Society is dead and died. There are people 'who give dinners' and people 'who give balls'. That is all. It is open to you to choose whether you will go or not, as you please. This was not the case when society existed. Then, you could no more refuse than you could refuse to dine with your Colonel. Either you were 'in society' – and in which case you kept to its rules, quite simply – or, you were not in society, in which case . . . you were considered to be some sort of swindler; or to have disgraced yourself.

Researching Female Aristocrats

It is much easier to research upper-class women than those who lived less public lives, as they are far more likely to appear in print or have left wills behind. Aristocratic women were also a highly literate class, and many even published their writing. Search the British Library catalogue or try the *Oxford Dictionary of National Biography* for these.

- *Oxford Dictionary of National Biography*: Notable upper-class women are often recorded in this. It gives a short biographical overview of the individual, as well as many intriguing details, such as biographies, books and sources for further research, portraits, wealth at death. Everyone has free access to the *ODNB* through their library card number. Simply log onto the website at www.oxforddnb.com (which is currently updated every year) to search over 57,000 individuals.

- **The National Portrait Gallery:** Notable women have long been immortalised with a place in the National Portrait Gallery. The first photograph of a woman ever acquired by the gallery was, interestingly, an image of Isabella Beeton. Search the collection online at www.npg.org.uk/collections/search.

- *Who's Who:* This is another useful online resource, and free to use, if you log on with your library card. It contains over 100,000 entries of 'the noteworthy and influential': www.ukwhoswho.com.

- *Burke's Peerage:* This famous directory contains over one million names of members of the peerage and gentry. Copies can be found in major libraries and some record offices. *Burke's Peerage* is also searchable online, but full entries are only available to subscribers, at www.burkespeerage.com.

- **Civil litigation:** As a class, aristocratic women had more possessions, and perhaps an independent income or inherited wealth. With greater resources, they were more often involved in litigation. Civil litigation means a dispute between two parties over issues like land, property, inheritance, debt and trusts. These cases were held in various courts until 1875. Finding out which court the case would have been heard in will make locating records much easier. Search The National Archives catalogue for litigants' names, but be aware that not all documents have been digitised yet. Records are also held locally, so try the relevant record office first.

- **County history:** Landowning gentry had a big effect on the surrounding land and villages. Take a look at local histories of the area, and the excellent Victoria County History of England website: www.victoriacountyhistory.ac.uk.

- **Family papers:** Aristocratic families' papers are generally well preserved, and upper-class women left behind letters, journals and account books, which all give a unique insight into their lives. Family papers or estate archives are held in local and county record offices, or large libraries such as the British Library and some university libraries. For example, the British Library holds Mary Gladstone's diaries and correspondence, and the Stanhope family papers are held at the Centre for Kentish Studies in Maidstone. Others are still in the possession of private individuals, but researchers may be granted permission to consult them. Try searching the National Register of Archives (www.nationalarchives.gov.uk/nra/default.asp).

Chapter 6

CRIMINAL WOMEN

In 1890, social investigator William Booth wrote about a nameless under-class living in 'Darkest England', with 'a population about equal to that of Scotland'. He estimated that 'three million men, women, and children' were enslaved by extreme poverty in the slums, common lodging houses and on the streets. Many, but by no means all, criminal women came from this class during the nineteenth century.

Women were drawn to crime between the nineteenth and early twentieth century for long-standing reasons: typically unemployment, destitution and poor education. Also, after prison doctors routinely began to examine

Alcohol addiction was blamed by many social commentators as a major cause of crime. It was easily available in gin shops, as pictured here in an illustration from Tom and Jerry: Life in London *(1822)*

prisoners in the 1860s, they discovered that 'large numbers . . . though not so bad as to be certifiably insane, were certainly mentally defective'.

Contemporaries saw criminality as stemming from alcoholism and immorality; vices that the poor and depraved passed on to their children. William Booth protested:

> The bastard of a harlot, born in a brothel, suckled on gin, and familiar from earliest infancy with all the bestialities of debauch, violated before she is twelve, and driven out into the streets by her mother a year or two later, what chance is there for such a girl in this world?

It was a dramatic view, yet it was to some extent true. In 1852, the recorder of Birmingham testified that children were trained to a life of crime, in a special commission on juvenile crime: 'They are hereditary criminals; they are trained to crime; they are practically taught to think light of it.' The Victorians considered female criminals as 'unnatural', 'even more morally degraded' and 'far more dangerous to society than the other sex', but it is difficult to calculate exactly how many women were involved in crime. In the late 1860s, female tramps, vagrants and prostitutes were excluded from criminal statistics – which shrank from 54,703 in 1860 to 11,445 in 1870. Yet, it is important to remember that only a small proportion of crimes were prosecuted and small misdemeanours – the sort of offences usually committed by women – were the least likely to come to court. The number of convictions in higher courts in England and Wales halved between 1850 and 1900 and the numbers given prison sentences fell from 14 per 100,000 in 1864 to just 2.5 by 1900. In the Edwardian era, the numbers were further reduced by the greater understanding of mental illness and alcoholism, as well as increased provision of therapy.

Destitute women take much-needed shelter for the night in a Salvation Army shelter, illustrated in The Graphic *in 1892*

Women were vulnerable to poverty, whether through the loss of a husband, unemployment or illness. Many, like this mother and her children, were forced into the workhouse

Girl defendants made up 5 per cent of cases in the new juvenile courts, in the first half of the twentieth century. Looking at case files from the Children's Society, historian Pamela Cox in *Gender, Justice and Welfare* discovered that many vulnerable young girls entered the prison system early, usually charged with minor offences, like petty theft. Twelve-year-old Ivy was charged by Southampton court in 1908 with stealing clothes from the workhouse where she lived, and was sent to an industrial girls' school in Oxfordshire.

As well as pauperism, drunkenness and 'inferior breeding', the fact that women were working was blamed by theorists for criminal behaviour. Rather, it was the instability of many women's professions that led individuals to crime: servants dismissed without warning, sweated workers on starvation rates and factory workers laid off when trade declined. A large proportion of Victorian women convicted of minor offences were noted as 'of previously good character'. Many of them were working hard to support themselves and fell into crime through desperation, with no one to turn to for help. The 1851 census revealed 365,159 'spare' women, and there were over a million more women than men in 1901. With a constant oversupply of female labour, employers could pay low wages. In York, in 1900, the average working-class man earned twenty-four shillings a week, while the average woman received ten shillings and ninepence.

Others had never learned a trade. In the 1840s and 1850s, 80 per cent of women arrested in Manchester had no respectable employment. One-third claimed to have 'no trade', another third were prostitutes and the rest described themselves variously as housekeepers, factory workers, domestic servants and charwomen, needlewomen – all unstable jobs. In Brixton Prison between 1853 and 1858, of 1,706 prisoners, 851 were recorded as 'entirely uneducated', 615 had learned to read and write in prison, fifty could read a little and just ten were 'tolerably educated' (the remainder were unrecorded). Once released from prison, poor women were often likely to return to crime or prostitution out of necessity – without skills or a reference they were unlikely to gain regular employment. Rosamund Hill wrote an article for the *English Woman's Journal* in April 1864, arguing that female convicts had a hard time gaining work when they were released: 'They are unable to perform the rough out-doors work for which no character is required. They must be domestic servants, or be employed in the factories; or if they work at home, they must be trusted with property; all three modes requiring . . . a good character.'

Where Were They Concentrated?

Crime rates have always varied enormously from place to place, but cities rather than towns were home to criminals in the nineteenth century. In rural areas, female crime rates were significantly lower and crime took on different forms – brawls between neighbours rather than random acts of violence, and stealing livestock as opposed to anonymous robbery. Although a few criminal communities existed in towns such as Merthyr Tydfil or Ipswich, like ordinary workers, criminals were drawn to – and created by – cities and the greater number of opportunities they could find there. Other towns and cities may have had larger proportions of criminals, but most offences were committed in the capital.

'London affords so many facilities for the concealment of criminality. The metropolis is like an immense forest, in the innumerable avenues of which offenders may always find retreat and shelter,' wrote John Wade in his 1829

London, with the biggest population of any English city, had dingy slums situated next to smart streets. The city always provided the most opportunities for criminals – and many of them were women

Treatise on the Police and Crimes of the Metropolis. In 1801, the population of London was almost a million – eleven times bigger than any other city – and the slums were just a step away from prosperous streets. In Covent Garden, brightly lit theatres stood right next to the Seven Dials slums; full of gin shops, 'flash-houses' (criminals' pubs), prostitutes, pawnbrokers, the notorious St Giles's Rookery separated fashionable shopping streets, Shaftesbury Avenue and Oxford Street.

London was not the only city with a thriving criminal community. The industrial revolution kickstarted the growth of factory towns, attracting high levels of migrants and creating higher crime figures. Liverpool, Bristol and Bath all had high numbers of juvenile criminals. Manchester, Birmingham and Leeds, too, had many 'part-time criminals' who supplemented their lawful wages with crime. Captain Willis, chief constable of Manchester told the *Morning Chronicle* newspaper, in 1849: 'There is a considerable floating criminal population in Manchester, a considerable fixed criminal population and a smaller number of persons who are known to both work and steal.' Manchester had a problem with gang violence. The population had exploded from 70,000 in 1801 to half a million by 1901, and during the mid-nineteenth century gangs of youths – some of them female – armed with knives and leather belts roamed the city's streets, attacking or 'scuttling' each other. Young mill-workers fought with clogs, boots, bottles, belts and knives.

Teeming, anonymous city slums provided the ideal setting for criminal activity. Andrew Mears, a Chelsea minister, protested: 'Entire courts are filled with thieves, prostitutes and liberated convicts. Who can wonder that evil flourishes in such hotbeds of vice and disease.' In the slum courts around

137

Bishopsgate and Aldgate in London, Mears continued: 'Instances are innumerable, in which a single room is occupied by a whole family – whatever may be its number . . . birth and death go on side by side; where the mother in travail, or the child with smallpox, or the corpse waiting interment, has no separation from the rest . . . men, women, and children in the promiscuous intimacy of cattle . . . every instinct of personal or sexual decency is stifled . . . every nakedness of life is uncovered there . . . I have seen mud larks sitting on the floor with baskets of filth before them, sorting out the occasional bit of coal or bone.'

What Were Their Crimes?

Women were not just perpetrators, but 'the accomplices of crimes, its aiders and abetters . . . the victims of crimes, and the seducers to crimes'. Thousands

Relatively few women committed major violent crimes, but murderesses always received a great deal of publicity, like servant Catherine Webster (pictured), who was executed for murdering her employer, Julia Thomas, in 1879

were involved in the criminal world at one remove – keeping market stalls as a cover for receiving stolen goods, running gangs of child thieves, procuring vulnerable young girls, and prostitutes leading their clients to be robbed by their pimp.

Equally, few female criminals committed major crimes. The nineteenth-century newspaper-reading public was thrilled by notorious cases involving young women. Twenty-two-year-old Madeleine Smith, tried for poisoning her lover in 1857; 16-year-old Constance Kent, dramatically reprieved of the death sentence for brutally murdering her young brother in 1865; and 18-year-old servant Sarah Harriet Thomas, hanged for bludgeoning her elderly employer to death in 1849. Yet, major female criminals were rare, and – excluding infanticide – women were convicted of roughly 15 per cent of murders during the Victorian period.

As late as the 1890s, Cesare Lombroso argued that certain physical features – skull size, thick body hair and wrinkles – indicated criminal tendencies in women, but having 'evolved less than men', women were less likely to commit crimes. Lombroso was right about one thing: female criminals did behave differently. During the nineteenth century, women were up in court for exactly the same offences as men, even the most brutal: 'drowning, battery, slashing with razors, gouging with knives, "dashing brains out" with pokers and cudgels, hacking with axes, stabbing with pitchforks'. But on the whole they committed fewer, less violent crimes than men, concentrating on certain types of offences such as those associated with sex and childbirth – brothel-keeping, prostitution, abortion and infanticide. They also stuck to various forms of theft – pickpocketing, prostitutes robbing clients, receiving stolen goods, counterfeiting coins – and made up one-third of convictions for drunkenness.

Prostitution

During most of the nineteenth century, the largest group of female criminals were prostitutes. In 1857, 28 per cent of women charged with a criminal offence were already working as prostitutes; 12 per cent in 1890. Not all were long-term prostitutes; many were on the streets as a temporary measure: servants, shop girls or widows struggling to make ends meet. Reverend G.P. Merrick, the chaplain of Millbank Prison, made notes on prostitutes he met in the prison. He found that of just under 15,000 women, 8,000 were domestic servants; 2,667 were needlewomen; 1,617 were in trade, shop assistants or factory workers; 1,050 were barmaids and waitresses; 838 were unemployed; 228 were in the theatre or music hall; 183 had been governesses and 166 were street-sellers. About 20 per cent of these women were still married, yet only 187 were still living with their husbands and many were widows.

Girls began selling their bodies on nineteenth-century streets before reaching their teens. Reverend Merrick discovered that, while most women

Many female criminals were also prostitutes, and many made more money stealing from clients than selling their bodies. Although these women are well-dressed, working at Kate Hamilton's brothel in the 1860s, the majority of women worked the streets

had been 'seduced' between the ages of 15 and 20, some had been as young as 11 or 12 when they first went on the streets. Until 1885, when it was raised to 16, the female age of consent was just 13. Sex with a virgin was believed to cure syphilis and even 'pillars of society' such as Conservative MP Cavendish Bentinck could get away with publicly stating that the rape was acceptable if money had changed hands: 'It is nonsense to say it is rape, it is merely the delivery as per contract of the asset virginity in return for cash down,' scoffed Bentinck.

A large proportion of the women that Reverend Merrick spoke to had made the decision to become a prostitute themselves. Of just over 16,000 he investigated:

5,061 voluntarily left to adopt 'a life of pleasure'
3,363 pleaded poverty and necessity from lack of employment
2,808 were led away by other girls
3,154 were seduced then drifted on to the streets
1,636 were betrayed under promise of marriage, then abandoned.

Prison inspector Mary Gordon discovered that many young prostitutes were paid in kind: 'from a pennyworth of sweets or a glass of beer to a cheap fur coat, fine box of chocolates or night in some hotel . . . Robbery from the person was perhaps their most profitable adventure. Some were really destitute vagrants.'

Prostitutes often doubled as small-time thieves, robbing their customers, especially drunken sailors or provincial visitors to the capital. They took money, gloves and watches from their client after he had undressed, while he slept, dipped into his pocket while soliciting, or lured him to a place where their pimp might appear to extort money from him. In 1837, Ellen Reece, a 24-year-old prostitute, was in Salford gaol awaiting a fourteen-year sentence of transportation. During her stay, the prison chaplain recorded some of her experiences. From the age of 14, she told him, she had 'lived entirely by prostitution or plunder. Seven times as much by robbery.' She proceeded to tell him exactly how: 'None of the girls think so much of prostitution but as it furnishes opportunities of robbing men . . . most girls will rob by violence and especially drunken men . . . [They] will not go to a house if they can help it; to some back street. Gentlemen notice the features so much better when you go to a house.' Whenever possible, Ellen took a client's wallet and escaped before she had to have sex with him. Ellen and her companion, Jane Doyle, would pick the client's pockets while his breeches were down and would run off while his state of undress hindered his pursuit. Sometimes they were arrested by the police, but Ellen and Jane had a variety of strategies to avoid being caught with the money:

> The places for hiding money are pockets in the underside of the Stays towards the lower part . . . wrapping it in a piece of rag or paper and putting it in the hair . . . Also, putting it where decency forbids to name – has known thirty Sovereigns hidden there at one time. Also swallowing it – has known eleven swallowed . . . If they don't get at it for two or three days they [prostitutes] get opening medicine.

Women like Ellen and Jane could be remarkably successful – until they were arrested. Relatively few of their victims wanted to publicise their visit to a prostitute, by complaining to the police. In 1886–7, the chief constable of Wolverhampton reported that thirty-eight such offences had been reported, but only eighteen were brought to justice. 'Complainants generally drunk – and following day decline to prosecute,' he noted. Grand juries also regularly threw out such cases if they did come to court, as there was a feeling that these men deserved to be robbed.

In addition to theft, prostitutes usually ended up in prison for drunkenness and disorderly conduct. At Liverpool, in 1842, the police arrested 2,899 'known prostitutes': 1,289 were charged with drunkenness and disorderly conduct, and another 528 with robberies from the person. Frequently arrested prostitutes 'regarded the ordinary arrest and fine as a kind of tax on their means of livelihood' and often had their bail paid by their pimps.

Few prostitutes had long careers or reached the upper echelons of their profession. Reverend Merrick wrote sadly:

> The rate of mortality among these poor creatures is terribly high . . . I find that the average number of years which they live after having taken to a 'life on the streets' is about three years and six weeks . . . Their being out in all weathers; their irregular hours, short and broken slumbers; their irregular meals, at one time starving, at another surfeiting; often only drink and no food at all; the constant drain on their natural strength.

In *Penal Discipline* Mary Gordon described how she believed that prostitution debilitated young women mentally, as well as physically:

> Some young girls who had been much knocked about . . . Some, when set going, romanced in the most remarkable way – I judged them to be suffering from extreme nervous exhaustion, but some may have been early cases of dementia . . . I noted that girls who become prostitutes at a very early age were not only exhausted and neurasthenic, but often appeared to remain infantile in voice and appearance, as though their development had been cut short . . . Syphilis in some of these cases, appeared to run a fulminating course. Hysteria . . . self-mutilation.

Few prostitutes left any records about their lives, but one wrote her life story in the 1820s, providing a warning to others and a compelling story. Elizabeth Kenning (sometimes spelled Kenyon) was born around 1790, and brought up in Chester. After leaving school, she moved to Manchester to work at a cotton factory, spending her evenings at 'dances, the theatre and any other places of public resort', and sometimes passing 'whole nights without any rest'. Flattered by 'false promises' and presents, she 'deviated from the path of virtue' and was seduced by a young man. 'After he had accomplished his vile own purposes, he grew tired, began to neglect me and looked very cool,' she recalled.

Elizabeth 'grew very desperate and determined on revenge . . . from the seduced I became the seducer'. She went to live in a brothel, where her new way of life gradually took its toll on her. After a customer beat her up, breaking two of her ribs, she became addicted to laudanum. Lacking a character reference and 'deprived of every means of subsistence', she was forced to remain 'haunted and unhappy' on the streets. Her nights became an endless round of dancing houses, drinking dens and 'nurseries of vice', often concluding in the house of correction.

She made a new start, working as a seamstress, yet 'temptation presented itself' through a handsome ex-lover. 'I had a great partiality for him . . . He knew my fondness too well . . . after having taken some liquor I was easily persuaded.' Deserted once more and driven back to the streets, she contemplated suicide. One evening, Elizabeth accosted a minister, who spoke kindly to her and encouraged her to attend church. Assisted by the congregation, she was admitted into the Liverpool Female Penitentiary at Edgehill in 1813. The penitentiary was one of many homes for fallen women established during the early nineteenth century; it aimed to rehabilitate prostitutes and return them to 'a respectable station in society'.

Elizabeth became a model inmate, but there was no chance of a new life for her. Paralysis spread throughout her body until she was entirely bedridden. In an entry for 16 May 1817, the penitentiary ladies' committee minute book records: 'EK having been 3 years in the house and being now quite helpless is allowed to continue on account of her exemplary conduct, which it is believed has a favourable influence on the minds of the other women.' Incapacitated, Elizabeth wrote religious poems and was eventually only able to hold a pen with her mouth. She died in the penitentiary in 1829, and the ladies' committee had her life story published.

Infanticide

Infanticide and concealing a birth were two of the most common crimes committed by women throughout the nineteenth and early twentieth centuries. Until 1803, a single woman who had concealed the birth of her illegitimate baby was automatically presumed guilty of infanticide if the child later died. Sensational infanticide cases received extensive press coverage, such as that of Mary Morgan, a 16-year-old maidservant in Presteigne, Wales, who severed her newborn baby's head with a penknife. In 1821, Hannah Halley, a 31-year-old cotton mill worker from Derby, gave birth at her lodgings. When her landlady heard the baby's cries, Hannah tried to hide it in a jug of hot water under her bed. The landlady found the child, which was horribly scalded, and when the baby died a few days later Hannah was convicted of murder and executed.

Between 1735 and 1834, ninety-seven other women were hanged for infanticide. Babies were poisoned, drowned, abandoned outside, crammed down the toilet and even had their throats cut. Some were probably stillborn, but even in the late nineteenth century women were sentenced to death for infanticide, although they were usually reprieved. Cases eventually prosecuted were just a small proportion of the real numbers. In Manchester, 124 children under 12 months old were found dead in bed in 1886, yet only four cases of infanticide were noted in police returns. Doctors often signed certificates without bothering to view bodies.

Desperate mothers who wanted to keep their children but couldn't care for them paid other women to look after their children. These 'baby farmers' were of varying quality, with some taking in large numbers and dosing infants with gin or laudanum to quiet them. Several shocking cases of neglect emerged throughout the nineteenth century: Annie Tooke, from Exeter, hacked her charge to pieces with an axe in 1879, and Margaret Waters from Brixton was executed in 1870 after she poisoned up to eighteen children and dumped their rag-wrapped bodies in the street.

Parliament responded by passing legislation designed to protect young children, for example the Infant Life Protection Act of 1897. This legislation demanded that parents registered the details of the foster carer with the local authorities, and set up inspectors to check their welfare. Later legislation in 1922 and 1938 removed the death penalty for the murder of a child under a year old, allowing the mother's mental disturbance as a defence.

Theft

'In London the trade of thieving may be properly compared to a game,' commented Edward Gibbon Wakefield, in 1831, in *Facts Relating to the Punishment of Death in the Metropolis*. He saw the game as one in which 'the player always wins until he loses all, and in which the average period during which a player will always win, is two years'. In the 1870s, women made up a third of convictions for larceny of under five shillings. Nineteenth-century female thieves tended towards small thefts – shoplifting bolts of cloth, tugging a handkerchief from a pocket, pledging stolen goods to pawnbrokers and prostitutes stealing from clients.

At the lowest level, women scraped a living picking up anything they could scavenge on the streets. On the Liverpool docks, women followed carts laden with bags of corn or bales of cotton on their way to the warehouses, ripping a hole in one of the bags and holding up their aprons to catch the contents. When they had all they could carry, they would crawl next to the cart as it approached the gate and creep out under the horses.

There was an entire underworld of thieving, with its own language. 'Gins' taught young thieves and screened them while they were practising; a 'picking-up woman' committed robberies in the street, then passed her haul to a male accomplice; and 'lady-wires' were pickpockets disguised as respectable women. Lady-wires caused unease among the public, who associated crime with dirt and disorder – now, any seemingly genteel woman could be a thief:

> The women travelling look so maidenlified and comely in their person, that no human being would suspect their being pickpockets . . . There are now in Manchester, three of the cleverest lady-wires travelling; one from Birmingham, one from Leeds and one from Liverpool. The oldest of these three is about 24, and the youngest about 16. This youngest keeps a young man, who is dressed like any gentleman . . . They look into the newspapers for intelligence about sales, and also about concerts,

which they attend, never going inside, but watching as the people come out.

Professional pickpocket Ellen Clarke recounted her career in the 1830s, while at Preston Gaol. At the tender age of 18 Ellen had been convicted along with her husband, John O'Neill, and her brother and sentenced to transportation. The authorities estimated that the gang had stolen around £3,000 over several years.

Ellen was born in Stockport, and from the age of 10 she had worked in a factory and had also been in service. By her early teens she noticed that her brother had begun to dress more finely than usual. He took her to Knoll Mill Fair and showed her the source of his new-found wealth: 'I stood before him so that nobody could see his hand while he picked a woman's pocket of 7s 6d.' Seeing this easy source of cash, Ellen took to thieving, and did remarkably well. 'I had been at a fair with another young woman only for a day and we got £3 between us . . . I went to Rotherham Statute Fair and got about £4.' She married John O'Neill, another thief, who 'taught me how to raise outside dresses and to pick inside pockets'. Joined by her brother Edward, the couple travelled around the country to fairs and public gatherings, punctuated by short prison sentences when they were caught:

We went to Hull and found Prince Albert was going to lay the foundation stone of Grimsby Docks. At Hull I got 17s. We went to Grimsby and Edward and I got 30s each. From Hull we went to Newark, where we got £7; then to Redford £4; then to Sheffield, where I was took up for 30s I had just taken from a woman. This bought me six weeks, and my husband two months in Wakefield . . . the largest sum I ever got was £22.

Despite their profits, Ellen was never content with her haul. O'Neill was a drinker and she paid 'from 20s to 35s a week to the beer-shop for him'. She would 'go out on Monday and get £2 and £3 which would satisfy me for two days, and then I would go again on Wednesday or Thursday and again on Saturday, and generally got in the week about £20. I was never satisfied with less.'

Stolen goods were 'fenced' and sold on through 'flash houses'. An 1816 Select Committee reported:

There are above two hundred regular flash houses in the metropolis . . . many of them, open all night: that the landlords in numerous instances receive stolen goods, and are what are technically called fences . . . many of houses are frequented by boys and girls of the ages of ten to fourteen and fifteen, who are exclusively admitted, who pass the night in gambling & debauchery, and who there sell and divide the plunder of the day, or who sally forth from these houses to rob in the street.

The Select Committee also reported how women acted as fences, many housing and encouraging child-thieves. In early nineteenth-century London, Mrs Jennings of Red Lion Market, in White Cross Street, was well-known:

This is a most notorious Fence & keeps a house of ill fame. She has secret Rooms by Doors out of Cupboards where she plants or secretes the property she buys till she has got it disposed of. Innumerable Girls & Boys of the Youngest class report to this House as she makes up more Beds & the House is thronged every night. She sanctions Robberies in her House which are continually committed by the Girls on Strangers whom they can inveigle into the House.

Women with barrows in markets and streets hid small objects, from silk handkerchiefs to hunks of cheese, passed to them by thieves, one at the corner of Gulston Street, in Whitechapel:

Puts handkerchiefs &c down her Bosom, and other things within her Barrow. She is known to all the little Cross Boys round the neighbour-hood of whom she will buy anything if she can only get a penny by it . . . she excited no suspicion from her situation with her Barrow, but it appears that this has become a very general practise with the lowest description of Fences.

A list of 'Notorious Harbours for Juveniles of Both Sexes' was compiled for Liverpool in 1856, and a selection makes sobering reading:

PB and wife, 4 children: This man and woman keep two houses, one for young thieves to sleep in, the other for receipt of their plunder.

SC and wife, 4 children, mother convicted: A notoriously bad place. Both had frequent robberies committed in the house. Juveniles induced to come there and fetch their plunder.

Mrs C, 2 children, thieving, mother in gaol: This woman excels in villainy. Her house is a second hell. Her children are now going in her track.

MC: A receptacle for young thieves. Her own daughter and herself one too.

JD and his wife, 4 children: The thieving propensities of this family have been handed down from father to son, on one side and from the

THE END OF THE PEARL CASE, MRS OSBORNE'S PRISON LIFE.

When Mrs Osborne was found guilty of jewellery theft in 1892, her new life in prison was imagined in detail by the press

mother's brood on the other side. Their house is a diabolical school for crime, and Van Diemen's Land is their utmost expectation.

Only 2 to 3 per cent of burglaries were committed by women – they were more often accomplices or lookouts. There were a few infamous exceptions, as the case of Sarah Lloyd, a maidservant barely out of her teens from Hadleigh in Suffolk. In 1799, Sarah was convicted of robbing her mistress then setting fire to her house, urged on by her lover Joseph Clark. Joseph was acquitted, yet despite the efforts of campaigners for a reprieve, Sarah was hanged.

Counterfeiting

Making counterfeit coins was a popular choice for female criminals. Women made up between one-third and a quarter of those charged with coining up to the end of the nineteenth century. It was a simple process, requiring just two workers. Sometimes the coiners were husband and wife; under contemporary law, if caught, the wife could plead that she had acted under her husband's direction and bore no criminal responsibility.

There were various offences associated with coining: making counterfeit coins; clipping coins to get metal for forgeries; colouring coins to make them seem of higher value; making counterfeit paper money; possessing counterfeit money or 'uttering', putting it into circulation; and possession of coining equipment. Counterfeit coin inspector at the Mint, John Field, revealed some of the tricks used by coiners: 'Plaster of Paris . . . is what are used to make counterfeit coin, and a good half-crown is used to make an impression on the mould . . . silver sand is used to polish the metal.'

In the eighteenth century, coining was a capital offence. In 1786, Phoebe Harris was burned at the stake for making counterfeit coins, followed by Margaret Sullivan and Christian Murphy, in 1788 and 1789. In 1790, hanging became the ultimate penalty for coining, and most, like Sophia Girton, convicted that year, were sentenced to death, later commuted to transportation. Women were still convicted for counterfeiting tiny values: Elizabeth Sedgewick, aged 19, was transported for life when she was convicted of coining a shilling at the Old Bailey in November 1832. Her mother, Mary Diggle, told the court that her daughter 'was decoyed away from home by bad companions'. As she was sent down, Elizabeth yelled 'My God! I am undone; I wish all the bloody curses may light on Bill Barrett, for learning me to make them!'

Louisa Baptiste was tried for falsely making and counterfeiting a half-crown at the Old Bailey in June 1856. Inspector William Penny raided Louisa's lodgings in Duck Lane, Westminster. In court, Penny reported:

> I saw the prisoner standing by a large clear fire. In her right hand she had a large plaster of Paris mould, in her left this large iron spoon, containing white metal in a fluid state. She put the spoon on the hearth, and at the same time laid hold of a counterfeit half-crown, with a get attached to it, off the mantel-piece, and put it into the iron spoon, which was quite hot, and the metal was in a fluid state. She at the same time dashed the mould on the floor, and commenced stamping upon it with her feet. Brannan then secured her.
>
> I produce three Britannia metal spoons which I found upon the mantel-piece, one partly melted, a file, the teeth of which were foil of metal, that was on the mantel-piece, also a piece of white metal. I also produce a piece of a mould which I found on the hearth quite hot, it was part of the one which she threw down and destroyed. She abused us very much, and said, 'You b—s you thought you had me to rights, but you b— you have not; if you had been here half an hour sooner you would; you ought to have been searched before you came here.

After she was brought to the police station, Louisa 'complained of great pain in her throat, and said that in the confusion, when the officers entered, she had swallowed a good half-crown'. She had to be taken to the hospital to

Capital punishment was used in fewer and fewer cases, but hangings always drew crowds, and in London people flocked to see female felons swing at Newgate (top) and Smithfield (bottom)

have it removed. Due to Penny's efforts, Louisa was sentenced to transportation for seven years.

What Punishments Were They Given?

From the seventeenth to the late nineteenth century, one in four defendants in criminal cases heard at the Old Bailey were female. In the early twentieth century this fell below one in ten, partly because minor theft cases were increasingly heard in lower courts. The Victorians considered that women's crimes were unnatural, against their 'gentle nature', but the women were often regarded with greater pity, unless they had committed serious crimes, and consistently received lighter sentences.

Old Bailey trial records reflect this. In a random sample of pickpocketing trials between January and April 1850, male defendants typically received harsher treatment, and usually prison sentences. Alexander Jackson, aged 19, got a year for stealing a handkerchief; and Joseph Martin, aged 17, eighteen months for stealing three shillings. But Ann Jones, aged 27, was confined for only four months for stealing a purse containing a sovereign, and three other female thieves – two of them also prostitutes – were found not guilty, in spite of strong evidence against them.

While fewer women were convicted, they were more likely than men to be 'hardened' criminals, with ten or more short sentences under their belt. The chaplain of Brixton Prison estimated in 1862 that 12 per cent of women there were reconvicted after release; in Liverpool 35 per cent were thought to re-offend. In 1900, 6,548 female and 4,176 male offenders had been convicted more than twenty times. Prison inspector Mary Gordon commented:

> Elderly or aged women who began in this way have been coming to prison practically all their adult lives, are to be found at all time in the prisons. There are women who have been convicted 20 or 30 times, before they were 20 years old. There are women whose convictions run into hundreds, or of whose convictions all count has been lost.

Mary Gordon explained the routine of a regular female prisoner:

> The woman arrives at the prison often in a very dirty condition. She is bathed, her clothing washed and fumigated, her hair cleansed, her skin diseases treated. If an old offender, she takes up her bucket or needle, where she laid it down last week . . . If she stays for a month or so she improves in health and usually puts on flesh. She gathers energy for her next debauch. She goes away, often only to return again – and yet again.

Prison

In the early 1800s, prisons were barely regulated, ramshackle, dank and ill-maintained; run at the whim of the gaolers, who doled out the best accommodation and food for bribes. If they had the means, prisoners could entertain prostitutes and guzzle gin. Ordinary prisoners received a penny-worth of bread a day, or a shilling-worth a week, but debtors had to survive entirely on charity and often starved to death.

These pre-Victorian gaols contained 'men and women, sick and healthy, sane and insane, veterans in crime, and youthful offenders gambled, drank, swore, concocted burglaries, and even manufactured counterfeit coin'. Prison reformer Elizabeth Fry visited the women's section of Newgate Gaol in 1817, and she found:

> The women were then mixed all together, young and old; the young beginner with the old offender; the girl for the first offence, with the hardened and drunken prostitute; the tried with the untried; the accused with the condemned; the transports with those under sentence of death; all were crowded together in one promiscuous assemblage; noisy, idle and profligate; clamorous at the gratings, soliciting money, and begging at the bars of the prison, with spoons attached to the ends of sticks.

However, after the 1823 Gaol Act introduced inspections, the new prison commissioners brought about an entirely new type of prison, with treadmills and cranks in male prisons, solitary confinement cells, the 'Silent System' and strait waistcoats for both sexes. The new model prison opened at Pentonville in 1842 set a precedent, with separate cells for each prisoner, heating and ventilation, a hospital, an exercise area and work-shops.

After transportation to the colonies ended in 1868, Britain's prisons had to accommodate more offenders. Younger prisoners began to be transferred to special juve-nile accommodation. By the 1870s, there were fifty industrial schools throughout the country housing 2,500 children, and sixty-five reformatory schools for 5,000 young offenders. The Borstal for girls held young women between 16 and 21 on short-term sentences, to avoid 'contaminating influences . . . degrading association of some of the older hands'.

What was life really like in prison? Local smaller prisons remained an odd mix of 'uncontrolled and dis-orderly people, the quarrelsome, the eccentric, the half

A female convict at Millbank Prison in 1862

A female convict at Wandsworth Prison in 1862

sane, all mixed together', yet larger prisons were well-regulated institutions. The inhabitants were varied. Prison inspector Mary Gordon classified them into several groups after a career in Edwardian women's prisons. There were women who committed serious offences 'usually frauds or thefts', with sentences of over six months. 'Sometimes they are accidental criminals, such as respectable servants or shop assistants. The smart punishment usually leaves them repentant, and they do not appear in prison again.' Others were 'expert facile thieves, and fraudulent persons, whose good manners, good speech and sometimes good education and nice appearance take in their victims over and over again . . . They often spend many years doing smart sentences.' There were also 'disorderly offenders . . . probably on account of their mental condition unlikely to change their habits . . . They are the vagabond confessed, and have accepted the police, the prison, themselves, their lives, for what they are.'

These women were 'by no means a meek and mild class' compared with male convicts. R.F. Quinton, a medical officer at Holloway Prison, wrote that 'violence frequently took on an epidemic form and too often the female pentagon was a pandemonium'. He added, 'Female criminals are not so filthy in their conversation with each other as men, but when they are in a state of excitement they will let loose torrents of abuse and obscenity.'

In December 1863, the chaplain of Bristol City Gaol recorded the havoc caused by four women confined together. Ellen S, 24; Emma M, 24; Mary Ann B, 41; and Elizabeth F, 18, were awaiting removal to Millbank Prison. Between 8 and 9pm:

> The three prisoners S—, M—, and F— began to sing and shout and call out to one another as loudly as they could. Upon being remonstrated with, they were very violent, and threatened to injure the female warders if they endeavoured to restrain them from 'having their fun out'. They proceeded to tear up their bedding, and threw a great portion

The female prisoners' clothing store at Tothill Fields Prison in 1862

of it into the yard below through their cell windows. The disturbance continued all night, and so threatening was their manner that it was considered desirable to send for one of the male officers to put their hands together in hand cuffs.

Mary Gordon wrote about bullying in female prisons: 'Taunting your fellow prisoner, which goes by the name of "crucifying" her, can also lead to trouble. In every prison, on almost every landing, is some woman who is recovering from the effects of drink, or who is excitable, hysterical or epileptic . . . On nearly every landing is the superior person prepared to "crucify" with looks and words.'

Dr Guy, medical attendant at Millbank Prison, complained of the difficulty in not being able to punish female prisoners by force:

As to the women who are given to tearing their clothes and smashing their windows, if they are put into a dark cell, they should shout and make merry. They know that there are prisoners not very far off them, who can hear their noise and they like to go on in that strange way; and

I think that if it were possible to inflict upon them some short bodily pain, it would be much more merciful.

He recorded that on average each prisoner at Millbank in 1861 had been punished twice:

Handcuffs – 52
Strait waistcoat – 403
Dark cell and minor punishments – 614
Admonishments – 647

Another method to prevent unruly behaviour was to keep inmates busy. The superintendent of Brixton Prison commented, in 1862, that 'female convicts, as a body, cannot bear to be idle . . . Unless actively employed they become restless and desponding and brood over the wretchedness their

Female prisoners sewing in Brixton Prison

Many Victorian female criminals learned to read and write for the first time while in prison

crimes have entailed on husbands and children.' Once set to work, many female prisoners 'turned out an amount of work that much exceeded any task that was likely to be set for them by the prison authorities'. Hard labour sounded draconian, but often it was laundry work, 'an exceedingly moderate day's work in scrubbing or the wash tub'. Of over 12,000 women in Holloway during 1908–9, only twenty-two were punished for idleness.

Some of the poorest women saw prison as a refuge. Mary Gordon realised that women prisoners referred to sentences of a few days as 'a wash and brush up' and would deliberately seek sentences long enough to last the winter, as prison was considered more comfortable than the workhouse. 'Here I can have a room to myself, and what with three meals a day, and the doctor whenever I want him, I'm better off here,' one told her.

A 'cell of one's own' was spartan, but clean, dry and heated. At Aylesbury Prison in 1900, cells were 'of ample size, and . . . lighted by long narrow windows covered with iron gauze'. While they seemed bare and empty they were 'not actually uncomfortable'. Each one was furnished with 'an iron bedstead, a wooden shelf, and a stool . . . a coir mattress and pillow, sheets, three blankets and a rug'. Each woman was also allotted a toilet bucket, 'a tin plate and a pint measure for their meals, and a card of the prison regulations'.

The daily routine was strictly maintained. At Aylesbury:

WOMEN			
Sunday .	Bread, 6 oz. Margarine, ½ oz. Tea, 1 pt.	Boiled bacon, 3 oz. Pease pudding, 8 oz.	Bread, 6 oz. Margarine, ½ oz. Cocoa, 1 pt.
Monday .	Bread, 4 oz. Porridge, 1 pt.	Potatoes with milk, 20 oz. Bread, 2 oz. Cheese, 1½ oz.	Bread, 6 oz. Vegetable broth, Cheese, 2 oz.
Tuesday .	Porridge, 1 pt. Skim milk, 1 pt.	Vegetable broth, 1 pt. Bread, 4 oz. Cheese, 2 oz. Dumpling, 6 oz.	Bread, 4 oz. Porridge, 1 pt.
Wednesday	Bread, 2 oz. Porridge, 1 pt. Treacle, 1 oz.	Boiled bacon, 3 oz. Bread, 4 oz. Potatoes, 8 oz.	Porridge, 1 pt. Skim milk, 1 pt.
Thursday .	Porridge, 1 pt. Skim milk, 1 pt.	Coffee, 1 pt. Bread, 6 oz. Cheese, 2 oz.	Bread, 6 oz. Vegetable broth, Cheese, 2 oz.
Friday .	Bread, 2 oz. Porridge, 1 pt. Treacle, 1½ oz.	Boiled bacon, 3 oz. Bread, 4 oz. Potatoes, 8 oz.	Bread, 6 oz. Gruel, 1 pt.
Saturday .	Bread, 4 oz. Porridge, 1 pt.	Vegetable broth, 1 pt. Bread, 4 oz. Cheese, 2 oz. Suet pudding, 6 oz.	Bread, 6 oz. Skim milk, 1 pt.

(In addition to the above, a lunch consisting of 4 oz. bread and 1½ oz. cheese is allowed daily.)

Women often ate better diets in prison and the workhouse. This shows the meals available to women inmates of York institutions in 1901

The prison day begins early, for at six o'clock the great bell rings for the convicts to rise. At a quarter to seven breakfast is served, and about ten minutes earlier the officers go round, and begin to unlock the cell doors so that the women may come out and receive their rations – three quarters of a pint of cocoa with bread.

They return to their cells, where they take their breakfast, after which they make their beds and clean out their rooms until towards eight o'clock, when it is time to go to chapel . . . at eight-thirty the labour of the day begins. The women are marched off in detachments to the work-rooms or back to their cells . . . The hardest labour is the laundry work and perhaps the twine making; and the women employed at these have extra rations, namely, lunch of bread and cheese.

At different times during the morning, they exercise in the prison yard, always keeping the same distance, and no word being spoken. Twelve o'clock is the dinner hour . . . all meals being taken in the cells . . . Four times a week they have meat; mutton twice and beef twice; on other days they have soup or suet pudding, and always bread and potatoes . . . at half-past one the various companies march back to the work rooms.

They exercise again during the afternoon, returning to their various occupations until five o'clock, when they go to their cells for supper, which consists of tea and bread. Very little work is done after this. At

Female prisoners exercise with their babies at Wormwood Scrubs Prison in the early 1900s

six forty-five all labour ceases for the day, and on entering their cells the doors are finally locked on them for the night. They have this time to themselves, and most of them spend it in reading. Precisely at eight the lights go out.

Prisoners were rewarded for good behaviour, grouped into different levels, with the top tier, the 'Star Class', given slightly better conditions. All wore badges on their arms with the number of years they had to serve or 'L' for life, and 'LR' for 'parole licence revoked'.

Women were occasionally allowed to receive visitors in prison

Transportation

British prisoners convicted of more serious crimes began being transported to America in the 1700s. When this convenient system for reducing overcrowding in British prisons was disrupted by the American War of Independence in 1775, the authorities looked for a new place to offload what they saw as the dregs of society. The First Fleet sailed to New South Wales, Australia, in 1787, and women

Case Study: HMS Rajah

In April 1841, HMS *Rajah* set sail from Woolwich with 181 women and six children on board. They were bound for Hobart, the capital of modern-day Tasmania, then Van Diemen's Land – a notoriously tough penal colony. By the early 1850s, when transportation was abolished, around 66,000 British convicts had been shipped out to the island, where they made up over half the labour supply and were intended as wives for settlers. In 1828 there were five men for every woman in Van Diemen's Land.

Ship's surgeon James Donovan noted that many of the *Rajah* women 'appeared somewhat delicate', and several showed signs of mental illness. Before they sailed, two 'became outrageously violent' and, along with three others 'showing violent symptoms of derangement', they were removed from the ship. During the voyage, the hot, cramped conditions below decks shortened tempers, and three women were 'for a short time violent'. There were outbreaks of diarrhoea, which caused one death.

Equipped with fabric, coloured thread, tape and needles donated by the British Ladies' Society for Promoting the Reformation of Female Prisoners, the women occupied themselves by creating an enormous quilt. This would have been supervised by the few non-transportees, perhaps Matron Kezia Hayter. The quilt was made up of 2,815 separate pieces. Fifteen of the *Rajah* women were listed as former seamstresses, but small bloodstains appear on the quilt, so others less skilled may have also taken part.

The *Rajah* laid anchor in Hobart on 19 July. Charles Darwin, on his trip to the island five years before, had praised the 'bright yellow fields of corn, and dark green ones of potatoes', fields that the *Rajah* women were expected to tend. On arrival, the *Rajah* women's quilt was presented to the lieutenant-governor's wife, intended as a gift for the Ladies' Society. Today it is the only surviving transportation ship quilt in the world.

Among the women who may have helped to create it are the following, who were all tried at the Old Bailey between 1840 and 1841 and sentenced to transportation for as little as stealing a handkerchief worth sixpence (Mary Ann King, 21, sentenced to ten years):

- **Mary Donovan, 20, and Matilda Everson, 21:** convicted of stealing a jacket worth fourteen shillings and a crown piece – seven years each. Mary Donovan picked up David May, a sailor, in the street late at night. May decided to sleep with Mary's friend Matilda Everson instead, paying her eighteen pence. The two women made off with May's jacket while he was sleeping. But the enterprising sailor scoured the local public houses, soon discovering the two women drinking away the proceeds of his pawned jacket. At their trial Donovan and Everson blamed each other. Did they reconcile during the voyage?

- **Elizabeth Cleveland, 53:** convicted of throwing vitriol in a stranger's face – fifteen years. Elizabeth's neighbour Mary Ann Murphy told the court: 'I heard a little bit of a bother . . . a girl ask the man for his money . . . and say "Don't let him go, he wants to bilk her". The street door was a little way open . . . the prisoner got a handful of flour, and hove at him . . . he turned round to see what she was heaving at him, and then she chucked something right in his face. He hallooed out, "Oh murder, murder, I am blinded".' The victim, George Day, a Holborn cabdriver, said, 'It burnt my face all over, and I have lost the sight of my right eye, and the other is so affected I can scarcely see at a distance.' Cleveland claimed that she had been cleaning candlesticks and accidentally spilt the acid on Day.

- **Mary Joy, 17 (a repeat offender):** convicted of stealing a pair of boots from a 7-year-old child – ten years. The victim, Elizabeth Proctor, told the court: 'She said she would give me some apples and pears, and a pair of green boots . . . she gave me a farthing cake and she took me up and carried me . . . [then] she unlaced my boots and took them off . . . I went home without any boots.'

- **Eliza M'Clewen, 38:** convicted of burglarously breaking and entering – ten years. Eliza claimed that she was owed three weeks' wages and her employer had simply charged her to avoid paying. Her employer protested: 'She lived about a fortnight with me, as I had a girl ill, who went to the hospital, but I never heard talk of any wages at all. She never demanded a halfpenny of wages.'

- **Maria Wicks, 22:** convicted of counterfeiting a shilling – fifteen years. Inspector William Penny said: 'I saw the prisoner Wicks sitting on a bed, quite close to a large clear fire. Perkins was standing up by the fire with a mould in his left hand, and a saucepan full of hot metal in his right hand. He dropped both and Wicks called out, "Jem, you b—r, break it, you b—r, smash it." Perkins had the mould under his feet at the time, and ground it to powder . . . I lifted up a loose board on the landing, just outside the door, and found a mould there for a half-crown.'

convicts were transported as well as men. They were regarded as prostitutes, and had no protection from sexual abuse at the hands of male convicts and the ship crew. Back in England, people heard the story of the infamous *Lady Juliana*, which sailed to New South Wales with a cargo of female felons in 1789. Once at sea, the *Juliana* sailors took 'wives' among the women, and the story was reported in the British newspapers, with the ship nicknamed the 'floating brothel'.

Until the 1820s, many of those sentenced to transportation were held in hulks (large ships moored on the Thames) containing up to 500 convicts. Once on board, 'convicts were chained or confined in cramped holds where they suffered successively from the cold and damp, rough seas and, in the tropics, from unbearable heat. Food rations were meagre, medical provision minimal, and segregation of the sick virtually impossible.'

Elizabeth Fry campaigned to improve conditions on transportation ships in the early 1800s. She helped to outlaw the use of irons on women and to allow children under the age of 7 to accompany their mothers. But once the women arrived in the colonies they were vulnerable; there were three men to every woman, and there was very little employment for them. In 1821, a factory was opened in Parramatta to provide female convicts with work and shelter, but it came to be used as a 'quasi-brothel and marriage mart' by male settlers and convicts. Other women were sent into domestic service with settlers, but were equally open to maltreatment, often working on isolated farms. The factories became places of protection for many women and some deliberately committed crimes to return there and escape abuse or violence.

More women were sentenced to transportation than men convicted of similar crimes, to redress the shortage of women. Australian officials hoped that the female convicts would act as a civilising influence on the men, but one official concluded that 'the influence of female convicts is valueless upon male convicts; women of depraved character do them no good whatsoever'. Western Australia refused to take women transportees at all: 'The accounts from the other colonies . . . have given them the idea that all female convicts are alike; that they are all prostitutes and drunkards, and all the rest of it.' In the mid-nineteenth century, transportation was being increasingly questioned as a suitable punishment for convicts. In 1852, the governor of Van Diemen's Land refused to take any more convicts, and in 1867 the final load of British convicts was transported to Western Australia. The British government resorted to long-term imprisonment in England as the most severe punishment.

Reforming 'Darkest England'

In 1906, the typical female habitual offender was presented as 'quite hopelessly beyond control . . . heroine of a hundred convictions, whose life is a perpetual horror and a public scandal . . . only kept alive by repeated terms of imprisonment'. This was not strictly true. As the nineteenth century drew to a close, women in prison were on average older: in 1866, 29 per cent were under 21, but a decade later this was less than 10 per cent. Young offenders were placed in special reformatories, giving them the chance to train for another life and escape the cycle of poverty and crime.

In 1922, when Mary Gordon wrote her memoir of her career as a prison inspector, she remarked that just before the First World War, hardship and poor levels of employment had filled up women's prisons. Of those on short-term sentences, she estimated that over three-quarters had been convicted previously. Even before the suffragettes won the fight for a female vote, there was an atmosphere of growing respect towards ordinary working women that permeated even the underworld, especially after female police officers were introduced in 1919. With greater education and the introduction of the welfare state after the Second World War, women had somewhere to turn to – and could begin to take control of their own lives.

Researching Female Criminals

There are many resources for researching female criminals, but they can be located in frustratingly far-flung sources, and access to more recent archive material is often restricted. While there is no automatic closure period, many court and police records close files for up to seventy-five years. Closure periods vary according to the type of material, who created it, and the regulations of individual records offices. However, since trials were often reported in the newspapers, there are still ways of finding out about cases, or supplementing archive material. Check the census, as women may appear residing in a prison.

- **The *Annual Register*:** From 1758 until the middle of the nineteenth century, this yearly publication included lengthy accounts of trials, from smaller church courts to major criminal courts. Infamous cases are covered in depth, for instance, the 1803 volume covers the case of Eliza Frances Robertson, nicknamed the 'female swindler of Blackheath'.

- **The 'Black Sheep' Index:** This incredibly useful website (www.blacksheep index.co.uk) has an index of half a million people mentioned in nineteenth-century newspaper crime reports. You can search for someone by name, view basic details, then order the full report on them for a fee, or use the information in the index to search the newspapers to discover more yourself.

- **The National Archives:** The archive at Kew holds records from four different courts: the Crown Court, and its precursor, the Assizes, which sat around the country, (in series ASSI; Crown Court, from 1972); the Central Criminal Court or the Old Bailey; and the Court of the King's Bench (usually for civil trials and abolished in 1875). The records consist of several categories: minute books and indictments (which give the charge, verdict and sentence) depositions (witness statements) and prison calendars (which have one-line entries on prisoners and can also give previous convictions).

The National Archives holds the criminal registers for England and Wales in series HO 27/63, which give details of criminal conviction and sentence. There is also a range of other documents such as petitions to the Home Secretary and appeals (series HO 17, 18, 19). These often contain riveting details, as sometimes the prisoners recount their life stories or retell the circumstances of their crime, and there might be testimonies from others as well as the decision. Series J 82 contains the records of the Court of Appeal from 1945 onwards.

There are also: records on individual prisons and women's prison licences (series PCOM 4); the *British Trials* penny pamphlets of court reports from 1867 to 1900 on microfilm; Metropolitan Police files in the MEPO series; and records on transportation to Australia from 1787 to 1867 (in series HO 11).

- **The *Newgate Calendar*:** Accounts of famous trials – often in lurid detail – were published from around 1700 to 1820, inspired by the bulletin produced by the keeper of Newgate Prison in London. There were many spin-offs after the first five-volume edition, including Andrew Knapp and William Baldwin's new illustrated edition, published in 1824 and 1826. You can find copies at large libraries and university libraries, and www.pascalbonenfant.com/18c/ newgatecalendar has a searchable database including data from various editions.

- **Newspapers:** These are an invaluable source of information on criminals, especially if they were involved in a sensational trial. The British Library's Colindale Newspaper Library in North London (The British Library, Colindale Avenue, London NW9 5HE) has a large range of resources: all UK national daily and Sunday newspapers from 1801, most provincial UK newspapers and selected foreign newspapers.

You can find evocative physical descriptions of criminals in newspaper reports. Consult nineteenth-century newspapers, local as well as national, online through the British Library's searchable archive at http://newspapers .bl.uk/blcs. Currently you have to pay for home access, but some UK libraries, universities and institutions such as The National Archives provide free access.

You can search *The Times* digital archive online (http://archive.timesonline .co.uk), although the site does charge for access. Check whether your local library subscribes to it.

The SOLON database of crime reportage (1850–90) hosted by Plymouth University (www.ssb.plymouth.ac.uk/JP/Solon/solondb.htm) is a great free resource.

The online John Johnson Collection of printed ephemera – from popular prints and advertising to pamphlets on crimes, murders and executions – held at the

Bodleian Library in Oxford is free when used through UK universities, further education institutions, schools and public libraries (http://johnjohnson .chadwyck.co.uk).

- **The Old Bailey Online:** This fascinating resource covers 210,000 trials held at the Central Criminal Court between 1674 and 1913. These shorthand notes relating to each trial have been digitised and are searchable online at www.oldbaileyonline.org by name or keyword. The National Archives holds the Old Bailey records from 1834, and London Metropolitan Archives all records before that.

- **Quarter sessions** (replaced by Crown Courts in 1972): These records are held by the county archives. Quarter sessions were held four times a year and dealt locally with less serious crimes. All of these records are indexed and you can search for them using the Access to Archives database (www.nationalarchives .gov.uk/a2a).

- **Transported criminals:** Registers of convicts in prison hulks and in prisons are in series HO 8 at The National Archives. These quarterly returns of prisoners' details include sworn lists of convicts on board the hulks (until 1861) and in convict prisons (from 1848), and criminal lunatic asylums (from 1862). They list prisoners' ages, convictions and sentences, health and behaviour. Check out The National Archives research guides on transportees sent to Australia and America at http://tinyurl.com/338j6jp.

  For convicts sent to Australia: The Convicts to Australia Database (at www.convictcentral.com) is searchable by ship name, and shows details about the transportation ship journey, like the date of arrival, ship's surgeon and number of passengers. The State Library of Queensland also has an online database of convict transportation registers (www.slq.qld.gov.au/info/fh/ convicts).

  For transportees to Tasmania: The Archives Office of Tasmania has an online convict index (http://portal.archives.tas.gov.au) which provides information on convicts once they arrived in Australia. If you have a convict's name, the name of the ship that they sailed on and an approximate date of arrival, then you will be able to find their convict number and locate relevant digitised records.

Useful archives:

Local archives and record offices hold records for the surrounding area, for example, magistrates', police court or petty sessions records, and these should be your first port of call. Try searching the Access to Archives website to pinpoint the location of relevant holdings or to find out where the records of particular institutions are held.

The Borthwick Institute for Archives, at York University holds records relating to Church courts, from the fifteenth to the twentieth century, and a wealth of case papers (University Library & Archives, University of York, Heslington, York YO10 5DD; www.york.ac.uk/library/borthwick).

The Galleries of Justice in Nottingham hold a fascinating range of archival material, as well as an excellent museum. They have the HM Prison Service Archive, a London Police Court Mission collection, and holdings from the Associated Societies for the Protection of Women and Children, in addition to many other documents on prisons and transportation (Galleries of Justice Museum, The Lace Market, Nottingham NG1 1HN; www.galleriesofjustice .org.uk).

The London Metropolitan Archives hold various law and order records spanning Westminster, Middlesex and the City of London from 1549 (40 Northampton Rd, London EC1R 0HB; http://tinyurl.com/5sykao).

The Open University Police Collection contains papers from private individuals as well as material from the City of London Police, photograph albums, cuttings, the *Police Gazette* and artefacts. You can arrange a research visit by making an appointment with the archivist (email: library-archive@open.ac.uk or telephone 01908 653378; The Library and Learning Resources Centre, The Open University, Walton Hall, Milton Keynes, MK7 6AA).

The Charles Booth Archive at the London School of Economics contains the original records from Booth's survey into *The Life and Labour of the People in London* from 1886 to 1903. You can search the collection online (at http://booth.lse.ac.uk) or arrange to visit (Archives Division, British Library of Political and Economic Science, London School of Economics and Political Science, 10 Portugal Street, London WC2A 2HD).

The National Library of Wales holds indexed court records for the Welsh Court of Great Sessions 1730–1830 (The National Library of Wales, Aberystwyth, Ceredigion, Wales SY23 3BU; www.llgc.org.uk).

BIBLIOGRAPHY

General

Barker, Hannah and Elaine Chalus (eds), *Women's History: Britain, 1700–1850: An Introduction* (Routledge, 2005).

Beddoe, Deirdre, *Back to Home and Duty: Women Between the Wars, 1918–1939* (Pandora, 1989).

Burnett, John (ed.), *Destiny Obscure: Autobiographies of Childhood, Education and Family from the 1820s to the 1920s* (Allen Lane, 1982).

Chapman, Colin, *Marriage Laws, Rites, Records and Customs* (Lochin Publishing, 1997).

Crawford, Elizabeth, *The Women's Suffrage Movement: A Reference Guide 1866–1928* (Routledge, 2000).

Creaton, Heather, *Victorian Diaries: The Daily Lives of Victorian Men and Women* (Mitchell Beazley, 2001).

Dyhouse, Carol, *Girls Growing up in Late Victorian and Edwardian England* (Law Books, 1980).

Gillis, John R., *For Better, for Worse: British Marriages 1600 to the Present* (Oxford University Press, 1985).

Hill, Bridget, *Women Alone: Spinsters in England 1650–1850* (Yale University Press, 2001).

Holcombe, Lee, *Wives and Property* (University of Toronto Press, 1983).

Jalland, Pat, *Women, Marriage and Politics 1860–1914* (Clarendon Press, 1986).

Lewis, Jane, *Women in England 1870–1950: Sexual Divisions and Social Change* (Indiana University Press, 1984).

May, Trevor, *An Economic and Social History of Britain, 1760–1970* (Longman, 1987).

Roberts, Elizabeth, *A Woman's Place: An Oral History of Working-Class Women 1890–1940* (Basil Blackwell, 1984).

Rowntree, Benjamin Seebohm, *Poverty: A Study of Town Life* (Macmillan, 1901).

Royston Pike, E. (ed.), *Human Documents of the Age of the Forsytes* (Victorian Book Club, 1972).

Sharpe, Pamela, *Working Women in the English Economy, 1700–1850* (Macmillan, 1995).

Steinbeck, Susie, *Women in England 1760–1914: A Social History* (Phoenix, 2004).

Stone, Lawrence, *Road to Divorce: England 1530–1987* (Oxford University Press, 1990).

Ward, Margaret, *The Female Line: Researching Your Female Ancestors* (Countryside Books, 2003).

Young, G.M., *Early Victorian England 1830–1865* (Oxford University Press, 1935).

Periodicals

Cornhill Magazine

English Woman's Journal

The Link

The Woman Worker (1907–10; 1916–21, produced by the National Federation of Woman Workers).

Women's Industrial News (1895–1919)

Women's Union Journal (1876–90, later replaced by *Women's Trade Union Review*, 1891–1919, although both were run by the Women's Provident League.

All of the above can be found in the British Library and the Fawcett Library. Other periodicals which ran articles on women's work included *The Englishwoman's Review*, as well as popular nationwide publications, like *The Graphic* and the *Illustrated London News*.

Domestic Servants

Davidoff, Leonore and Ruth Hawthorn, *A Day in the Life of a Domestic Servant* (Allen & Unwin, 1976).

Dickens, Monica, *One Pair of Hands* (Michael Joseph, 1939).

Ebery, Mark, *Domestic Service in Late Victorian and Edwardian England 1871–1914* (University of Reading, 1976).

Girouard, Mark, *Life in the English Country House: A Social and Architectural History* (Yale University Press, 1993).

Hill, Bridget, *Servants: English Domestics in the Eighteenth Century* (Clarendon Press, 1996).

Horn, Pamela, *The Rise and Fall of the Victorian Servant* (Macmillan, 1975).

—— *My Ancestor Was In Service* (Society of Genealogists, 2009).

May, Trevor, *The Victorian Domestic Servant* (Shire Publications, 1998).

Musson, Jeremy, *Up and Down Stairs: The History of the Country House Servant* (John Murray, 2009).

Paterson, Michael, *A Brief History of Life in Victorian Britain: A Social History of Queen Victoria's Reign* (Constable & Robinson, 2008).

Powell, Margaret, *Below Stairs* (Peter Davies, 1968).

Sambrook, Pamela, *Keeping Their Place: Domestic Servants in the Country House 1700–1920* (Sutton Publishing, 2005).

—— *A Country House at Work: Three Centuries of Dunham Massey* (National Trust, 1999).

Steedman, Carolyn, *Labours Lost. Domestic Service and the Making of Modern England* (Cambridge University Press, 2009).

Terry, Judith, 'Seen But Not Heard: Servants in Jane Austen's England', *Persuasions*, vol. 10 (1988).

Primary Sources

Adams, Samuel and Sarah Adams, *The Complete Servant* (1825).

Anon, 'Modern Domestic Service', *Edinburgh Review* (April 1862).

Butler, C.V., *Domestic Service. An Enquiry by the Women's Industrial Council* (G. Bell, 1916).

Davey, Dolly, *A Sense of Adventure* (SE1 People's History Project, 1980).

Fakenham Institution for Training Girls for Domestic Service and Orphanage, *Report for 1873* (T.J. Miller, 1874).

Fremlin, Celia, *The Seven Chars of Chelsea* (Methuen, 1940).

Gibbs, Rose, *In Service: Rose Gibbs Remembers* (Archives for Bassingbourn and Camberton Village College, 1981).

Hall, Edith, *Canary Girls and Stockpots* (W.E.A. Luton, 1977).

Harrison, Rose, *Rose: My Life in Service* (Littlehampton, 1975).

Jermy, Louise, *Memoirs of a Working Woman* (Goose & Son, Norwich, 1934).

Moulder, P.E., 'The General Servant Problem', *Westminster Review*, vol. 150 (August 1903).

Panton, J.E., *From Kitchen to Garret* (1890).

Agricultural Labourers

Horn, Pamela, *Labouring Life in the Victorian Countryside* (Sutton, 1976).

Langlands, Alex, Peter Ginn and Ruth Goodman, *Victorian Farm* (Pavillion Books, 2009).

Mingay, G.E., *Rural Life in Victorian England* (Sutton, 1998).

Owen, Christabel S., *History of British Agriculture 1846–1914* (Longman, 1964).

Pinchbeck, Ivy, *Women Workers and the Industrial Revolution 1750–1850* (Virago, 1981 edition).

Sayer, Karen, 'Field-Faring Women: The Resistance of Women who Worked in the Fields of Nineteenth-Century England', *Women's History Review*, vol. 2, no. 2 (1993).

Verdon, Nicola, *Rural Women Workers in Nineteenth-Century England: Gender, Work and Wages* (Boydell Press, 2002).

Waller, Ian, *My Ancestor Was an Agricultural Labourer* (Society of Genealogists Publications, 2010 second edition).

West, John, *Village Records* (Phillimore, 1982).

Primary Sources

Parliamentary Reports

Ministry of Reconstruction, *Report of the Women's Employment Committee* (HMSO, London, 1919).

Reports of Special Assistant Poor Law Commissioners of the Employment of Women and Children in Agriculture (HMSO, 1843).

Reports of Special Assistant Poor Law Commissioners of the Employment of Women and Children in Agriculture 1867–8 (HMSO, 1868).

White, J.E., *Report on the Agricultural Gangs in the Counties of Norfolk, Suffolk, Cambridgeshire, Northamptonshire, and Nottinghamshire* (HMSO, 1867).

Memoirs and Contemporary Accounts

Burlend, Rebecca, *A True Picture of Emigration* (Lakeside Press, 1936).

Cobbett, William, *Cottage Economy* (C. Clement, 1822).

Lee, Robert, *Unquiet Country: Voices of the Rural Poor 1820–1880* (Windgather Press, 2006).

Munby, Arthur and Derek Hudson (eds), *Munby – Man of Two Worlds: The Life and Diaries of Arthur J Munby 1828–1910* (John Murray, 1972).

Reay, Barry, *Rural Englands: Labouring Lives in the Nineteenth Century* (Palgrave Macmillan, 2008).

Rider Haggard, Henry, *Rural England: Being an Account of Agricultural and Social Researches* (Longmans Green, 1902).

Savory, Arthur H., *Grain and Chaff from an English Manor* (Oxford, 1920).

Skinner, John, 'Wages and Conditions of Women and Children Employed in Agricultural Labour in England: Effect of that Condition and Description of Labour on Their Health and Morals', *Monthly Journal of Agriculture*, vol. 1, (July 1845).

Taylor, Kate, in Burnett, John (ed.), *Destiny Obscure: Autobiographies of Childhood, Education and Family from the 1820s to the 1920s* (Allen Lane, 1982).

Thompson, Flora, *Lark Rise to Candleford* (Oxford University Press, 1939).

Factory Workers

Gray, Robert, *The Factory Question and Industrial England, 1830–1860* (Cambridge University Press, 1996).

Pinchbeck, Ivy, *Women Workers and the Industrial Revolution 1750–1850* (Virago, 1981 edition).

Primary Sources

Abram, W.A., 'Social Condition and Political Prospects of the Lancashire Workmen', *Fortnightly Review* (October 1868).

Anderson, Adelaide Mary, *Women in the Factory. An Administrative Adventure* (John Murray, 1922).

Bell, Florence, *At the Works: A Study of a Manufacturing Town* (Edward Arnold, 1907).

Black, Clementina, *Married Women's Work* (Women's Industrial Council, 1915).

Booth, Charles, *Labour and Life of the People* (Macmillan and Co., 1889–1891).

Eden, F.M., *The State of the Poor* (1797).

Farningham, Marianne, *A Working Woman's Life* (James Clarke, 1907).

Foley, Alice, *A Bolton Childhood* (Manchester University Press, 1973).

Gaskell, P., *The Manufacturing Population* (Baldwin and Craddock, 1833).

Hall, Edith, *Canary Girls and Stockpots* (W.E.A. Luton, 1977).

Higgs, Mary, *The Housing of the Woman Worker* (1915).

Kingsley, Charles, *Cheap Clothes and Nasty* (1850).

Merryweather, Mary, *Experience of Factory Life: Being a Record of Fourteen Years' Work at Mr Courtauld's Silk Mill at Halstead, in Essex* (Emily Faithfull, 1862).

Waugh, Edwin, *Home-Life of the Lancashire Factory Folk During the Cotton Famine*, (Simpkin, Marshall & Co., 1867).

Webb, Beatrice, *The Case for the Factory Acts* (Grant Richards, 1901).

Parliamentary Reports

Children's Employment Commission, First Report (vol. 18, 1863).

Children's Employment Commission, Third Report (vol. 22, 1864).

Children's Employment Commission, Fourth Report (vol. 20, 1865).

Factory Commissoners' Supplementary Report (vol. 27, 1834).

Ministry of Reconstruction, *Report of the Women's Employment Committee* (HMSO, London, 1919).

Report of the Select Committee on Factory Children's Labour (vol. 15, 1832).

Third Report of the Select Committee of the House of Lords on the 'Sweating System' (vol. 13, 1889).

Middle Classes

Bostridge, Mark, *Florence Nightingale: The Woman and Her Legend* (Viking, 2008).

Branca, Patricia, *Silent Sisterhood: Middle Class Women in the Victorian Home* (Croom Helm, 1975).

Copelman, Dina M., *London's Women Teachers: Gender, Class and Femininity 1870–1930* (Routledge, 1996).

Delgado, Alan, *The Enormous File: A Social History of the Office* (John Murray, 1977).

Dyhouse, Carol, *Girls Growing Up in Late Victorian and Edwardian England* (London, Routledge, 1981).

Fraser, Flora, *The English Gentlewoman* (Barrie & Jenkins, 1987).

Higgs, Michelle, *Life in the Victorian Hospital* (History Press, 2009).

Hughes, Kathryn, *The Victorian Governess* (Hambledon Press, 1993).

Jackson, Alan A., *The Middle Classes, 1900–1950* (David St John Thomas, 1991).

Liddington, Jill, *Rebel Girls: Their Fight for the Vote* (Virago, 2006).

Messenger, Sharon Ann, Thesis: 'The Life-Styles of Young Middle-Class Women in Liverpool in the 1920s and 1930s' (University of Liverpool, September 1998).

Pearsall, Ronald, *Edwardian Life and Leisure* (David & Charles, 1973).

Purvis, June, *A History of Women's Education in England* (Open University, 1991).

—— *Hard Lessons: The Lives and Education of Working Women in Nineteenth-Century England* (Polity Press, 1993).

Widdowson, F., *Going Up into the Next Class: Women and Elementary Teacher Training 1840–1914* (Women's Research and Resources Centre, 1980).

Primary Sources

Anon, *Governess Life: Its Trials, Duties, and Encouragements* (John W. Parker, 1845).

Anon, *Manners and Rules of Good Society* (1888).

Blackmore, Helen (ed.), *A Handbook for Women Engaged in Social and Political Work* (Edward Stanford, 1895).

Memoirs and Biographies

Chorley, Katharine, *Manchester Made Them* (Faber and Faber, 1950).

Edgecumbe, Fred (ed.), *Letters of Fanny Brawne to Fanny Keats* (Oxford University Press, 1936).

Farningham, Marianne, *A Working Woman's Life* (James Clarke & Co., 1907).

Furse, Katharine, *Hearts and Pomegranates: The Story of Forty-Five Years 1875 to 1920* (Peter Davies, 1940).

Gaskell, Elizabeth, *Private Voices: The Diaries of Elizabeth Gaskell and Sophia Holland*, edited by J. Chapple and Anita Wilson (Keele University Press, 1996).

Gavin, Adrienne E., *Dark Horse. A Life of Anna Sewell* (Sutton, 2004).

Macmanus, Emily E., *Matron of Guy's* (Andrew Melrose, 1956).

Mostyn Bird, M., *Woman at Work: A Study of the Different Ways of Earning a Living Open to Women* (Chapman and Hall, 1911).

Ness Macbean Ross, Elizabeth, *A Lady Doctor in Bakhtiari Land*, edited by James MacBean Ross (1921).

Neville, Lady Dorothy, *My Own Times* (Methuen, 1912).

Raverat, Gwen, *Period Piece: A Cambridge Childhood* (Faber and Faber, 1952).

Sewell, Elizabeth (ed.), *The Autobiography of Elizabeth Sewell* (Longmans, Green and Co., 1907).

Stephens, Sarah, *Passages From the Life of a Daughter at Home* (1845, reprinted by Kessinger, 2010).

Swanwick, Helena, *I Have Been Young* (Victor Gollancz, 1935).

Vincinus, Martha, *Independent Women: Work and Community for Single Women 1850–1920* (Virago, 1985).

Whiteing, Eileen, *Anyone for Tennis: Growing up in Wallington between the Wars* (London Borough of Sutton Libraries and Arts Services, 1979).

Aristocrats

Cannadine, David, *The Decline and Fall of the British Aristocracy* (Yale University Press, 1990).

Rees, Barbara, *The Victorian Lady* (Gordon & Cremonesi, 1977).

Reynolds, K.D., *Aristocratic Women and Political Society in Victorian Britain* (Clarendon Press, 1998).

Tweedsmuir, Susan, *The Edwardian Lady* (Duckworth, 1966).

Primary Sources

Birchall, D. and E. Birchall, *The Diary of a Victorian Squire: Extracts from the Diaries and Letters of Dearman and Emily Birchall*, edited by David Verey (Alan Sutton, 1983).

Cardigan, Countess of, *My Recollections* (Eveleigh Nash, 1909).

Colin Campbell, Gertrude, *Etiquette* (Cassell, 1893).

Greville, Violet, *The Gentlewoman in Society* (Henry and Co., 1892).

Loudon, Mrs, *The Lady's Country Companion or, How to Enjoy a Country Life Rationally* (London, 1845).

Miles, Alice Catherine, *Every Girl's Duty: the Diary of a Débutante*, edited by Maggy Parsons (Andre Deutsch, 1992).

Neville, Dorothy, *My Own Times* (Methuen, 1912).

Power Cobbe, Frances, *The Life of Frances Power Cobbe by Herself* (Richard Bentley and Son, 1894).

Tayler, William; Wise, Dorothy (ed.), *The Diary of William Tayler, Footman* (Westminster City Archives, 1998).

Twining, Louisa, *Recollections of Life and Work, Being the Autobiography of Louisa Twining* (Edward Arnold, 1893).

Criminal Women

Clark, Richard, *Women and the Noose: A History of Female Execution* (Tempus, 2007).

Cox, Pamela, *Gender, Justice and Welfare: Bad Girls in Britain, 1900–1950* (Palgrave Macmillan, 2003).

Jones, David, *Crime, Protest, Community and Police in Nineteenth-Century Britain* (Routledge & Kegan Paul, 1982).

Low, Donald A., *Thieves Kitchen: The Regency Underworld* (J.M. Dent & Sons Ltd., 1982).

Philips, David, *Crime and Authority in Victorian England: The Black Country 1835–1860* (Croom Helm, 1977).

Storey, Neil, *The Victorian Prison* (History Press, 2010).

Thomas, Donald, *The Victorian Underworld* (John Murray, 1998).

Tobias, J., *Crime and Industrial Society in the Nineteenth Century* (Pelican, 1972).

Weiner, Martin J., *Reconstructing the Criminal: Culture, Law and Policy in England 1830–1914* (Cambridge University Press, 1990).

Zedner, Lucia, *Women, Crime, and Custody in Victorian England* (Clarendon Press, 1991).

Primary Sources

Booth, William, *In Darkest England* (1890).

Carpenter, Mary, *Our Convicts* (Longman, 1864).

Gibbon Wakefield, Edward, *Facts Relating to the Punishment of Death in the Metropolis* (James Ridgeway, 1831).

Gordon, Mary, *Penal Discipline* (Routledge, 1922).

Johnston, M.F., 'The Life of a Woman Convict', *Fortnightly Review*, no. 75 (1901).

Kenning, Elizabeth, *Some Account of the Life of E K chiefly drawn up by herself* (Bradford, 1829).

Lombroso, Cesare, *The Female Offender* (Appleton, 1920).

Merrick, G.P., *Work Among the Fallen as Seen in the Prison Cell* (Ward, Lock and Co., 1891).

Quinton, R.F., *Crime and Criminals 1876–1910* (Longmans, Green & Co., 1910).

Useful Archives, Libraries and Museums

All of the following are good places to start your research or begin to explore women's history:

The Feminist Library
5 Westminster Bridge Road,
London SE1 7XW
020 7261 0879
http://feministlibrary.co.uk

The National Archives
Ruskin Avenue,
Kew,
Richmond TW9 4DU
020 8876 3444
www.nationalarchives.gov.uk

The People's History Museum
Left Bank,
Spinningfields,
Manchester M3 3ER
0161 838 9190
www.phm.org.uk

The Society of Genealogists
14 Charterhouse Buildings,
Goswell Road,
London EC1M 7BA
020 7251 8799
www.sog.org.uk

The Wellcome Institute
215 Euston Road,
London NW1 2BE
020 7611 8888
www.wellcome.ac.uk

The Women's Library
London Metropolitan University,
25 Old Castle Street,
London E1 7NT
020 7320 2222
www.londonmet.ac.uk/thewomenslibrary

A SHORT TIMELINE OF KEY EVENTS IN WOMEN'S SOCIAL HISTORY, 1819–1929

1819 – Queen Victoria is born.

1820 – Flogging is abolished as a punishment for female convicts.

1828 – The Offences Against the Person Act removes the death penalty for abortion.

1833 – The Factory Act makes the employment of women and children for over twelve hours a day illegal.

1834 – The Poor Law Amendment Act establishes workhouse unions and abolishes the Speenhamland system of outdoor relief.

1837 – Alexandrina Victoria, daughter of Prince Edward, Duke of Kent, becomes queen on the death of William IV.

1839 – The Custody of Infants Act gives mothers separated from their husbands the legal right to petition for access to their children and custody of children under 7 years old. Previously, women who left their husbands had no automatic right to see their children.

1840 – Queen Victoria marries Prince Albert of Saxe-Coburg and Gotha.

1842 – Chadwick's *Report on the Sanitary Condition of the Labouring Classes* reveals the squalor in which many working people are forced to live.
　　　Lord Ashley's Coal Mines Act prevents underground employment of women and boys under the age of 10 in the mines.

1847 – Charlotte and Emily Brontë publish *Jane Eyre* and *Wuthering Heights*.
　　　The Ten Hours Factory Act limits working hours for women and children.

1848 – Queen's College is founded to train women teachers, in London.

1850 – The Public Library Act is the first step in creating free public libraries for all.

1851 – A petition for women's suffrage is presented to the House of Lords by the Sheffield Female Political Association.

1853 – The Act for the Better Prevention and Punishment of Aggravated Assaults upon Women and Children increases penalties and allows third-party complaints.

1854 – Florence Nightingale's nurses arrive in the Crimea.

1857 – The Divorce and Matrimonial Causes Act widens access to divorce, making it possible without an Act of Parliament.

1861 – Isabella Beeton's *On Household Management* is published.

1864 – The passage of the Contagious Diseases Act (followed by more legislation in 1866 and 1869) allows police officers to take any woman suspected to be a prostitute off the street to be forcibly examined for sexually transmitted diseases.

1865 – Elizabeth Garrett becomes the first English woman to be included on the Medical Register.

1867 – The Manchester Women's Suffrage Committee is formed by Lydia Becker, followed by other regional committees and the National Society for Women's Suffrage.

1869 – JS Mill publishes *The Subjection of Women*.

Hitchin College for Women, the precursor for Girton College, Cambridge, is founded.

1870 – The Ladies' National Association for the Repeal of the Contagious Diseases Acts is founded by Josephine Butler.

Women are allowed to serve on school boards.

The Married Woman's Property Act allows women to keep the wages that they earn through their work (their earnings were previously the legal property of their husband). This is followed by more legislation in 1874, and 1882.

Forster's Education Act makes schooling (at least theoretically) available to all children up to the age of 10 (raised to 11, in 1893, and twelve in 1899).

1873 – The Infant Custody Act allows mothers to be granted custody of children aged up to 16.

1874 – The Women's Protective and Provident League is founded (later renamed the Women's Trade Union League).

1876 – All medical licensing bodies in the UK are forced to open their examinations to women, but are allowed to do so at their discretion.

1878 – The Matrimonial Causes Act means that judges and JPs can now grant judicial separation to a wife if her husband is convicted of aggravated assault upon her. In 1884 the Act is expanded to force husbands to pay maintenance if they have deserted their wives.

1881 – The Army Nursing Service is founded.

1886 – The Contagious Diseases Acts are repealed.

1889 – Lady Sandhurst is elected to the London County Council, but is not allowed to take her seat because she is a woman.

1891 – The case *Regina v Jackson* enshrines a woman's right to live apart from her husband, if she chooses to.

1892 – A quarter of a million people sign a women's suffrage petition, which is sent to Parliament.

1897 – The National Union of Women's Suffrage Societies is founded, with Millicent Fawcett as president, and amalgamates about 500 local societies.

1899 – Havelock Ellis's *Psychology of Sex* is published.

1900 – Charlotte Cooper becomes the first British gold medallist in the 1900 Olympics, in Paris.

1903 – Judges refuse to admit trained lawyer Miss Bertha Cave to the bar, as there is no legal precedent.

The WSPU is founded by Emmeline Pankhurst.

1905 – The first disruption of a political meeting by suffragettes, in Manchester.

1907 – The Qualification of Women Act enables women to sit as councillors, aldermen, mayors and chairmen on county and borough councils.

The Marriage to Deceased Wife's Sister Act allows a widow to marry her brother-in-law.

Free secondary school places are introduced for male and female students up to the age of 16.

1908 – The first female mayor is elected, Dr Elizabeth Garrett Anderson, at Aldeburgh, Suffolk.

Edith New becomes the first suffragette to chain herself to the railings outside 10 Downing Street.

1909 – Marion Wallace-Dunlop becomes the first suffragette hunger-striker.

1910 – The Girl Guides are founded by Robert Baden Powell.

1911 – Women's suffrage supporters boycott the census.

1912 – Harriet Quimby becomes the first woman to fly across the English Channel.

1913 – The Temporary Discharge Act, known as the 'Cat and Mouse Act' allows authorities to free ailing hunger-striking suffragettes from prison, then re-arrest them once they are well.

Emily Davidson dies at Ascot, throwing herself in front of the king's horse.

Emily Duncan becomes the first female magistrate, in West Ham.

The Women's War Register is set up and the Women's Land Service Corps is formed.

1916 – The Royal College of Nursing is founded.

1917 – Women begin to be employed on light duties behind the lines, in France.

1918 – The vote is granted to female householders over 30.

1919 – The first parliamentary election in which women can vote.

The Sex Disqualifications Removal Act legally allows women into trades and the professions.

1920 – The Women's Training and Employment Committee is set up to promote employment for women and help those affected by the war.

Women gain full membership of Oxford University.

1921 – The first women sit on a divorce court jury.

1922 – Infanticide becomes a statutory offence.

1923 – The Legitimacy Act means that parents are able to legitimise a child by marrying after its birth.

A new Matrimonial Causes Act allows wives to divorce husbands solely for adultery.

1928 – Woman aged 21 and over are granted the vote.

1929 – Female voters outnumber males at the general election.

Margaret Bondfield, Labour MP for Northampton, becomes the first female Cabinet Minister.

INDEX